An Introduction to Hegel's Logic

A great man condemns people to explicate him.

—*G.W.F. Hegel*

An Introduction to Hegel's Logic

Justus Hartnack

Translated from the Danish by
Lars Aagaard-Mogensen

Edited by
Kenneth R. Westphal

Hackett Publishing Company, Inc.
Indianapolis/Cambridge

04   03   02   01   00   99   98   1   2   3   4   5   6

Cover design by Deborah Wilkes
Interior design by Meera Dash

Library of Congress Cataloging-in-Publication Data

Hartnack, Justus.
     [Hegels Logik. English]
     An introduction to Hegel's logic / by Justus Hartnack : translated
from the Danish by Lars Aagaard-Mogensen : edited by Kenneth R.
Westphal.
         p.   cm.
     Includes bibliographical references and index.
     ISBN 0-87220-425-1 (cloth).—ISBN 0-87220-424-3 (pbk.)
     1. Hegel, Georg Wilhelm Friedrich, 1770–1831—Criticism and
Interpretation.
     B2948.H24513   1998
     160'.92—dc21   98–38163
                                                          CIP

The paper used in this publication meets the minimum requirements of
American National Standard for Information Sciences—Permanence of
Paper for Printed Library Materials, ANSI Z39.48-1984.
∞

Contents

Abbreviations of Hegel's frequently cited texts:

PS *Phenomenology of Spirit*, trans. A. V. Miller. Oxford: Clarendon Press, 1977.

SL *Hegel's Science of Logic*, trans. A. V. Miller. London: George, Allen & Unwin; New York: Humanities, 1969.

Enz. *The Encyclopaedia Logic*, trans. T. F. Geraets, W. A. Suchting, and H. S. Harris. Indianapolis: Hackett Publishing Co., 1991.

Note on Hegel's texts

Both the *Phenomenology of Spirit* and the *Science of Logic* are complete, self-standing texts. They are cited by page numbers. Hegel's *Encyclopaedia* is a lecture compendium divided into sections. To some sections Hegel appended published remarks. To most sections Hegel's editors have appended "additions" extracted from student notes taken from his lectures. Accordingly, Hegel's *Encyclopaedia Logic* is cited by section numbers; "Remark" indicates Hegel's own published remark; "Addition" indicates lecture material appended by Hegel's editors.

Preface

Why has this book on Hegel's logic been written? One reason can be found in the aphorism from Hegel's Berlin period cited in the epigraph. Even though the aphorism proposes a general rule, it is applicable *par excellence* to Hegel himself. Another reason can be found in what H. Sussmann has called the "Hegelian aftermath," by which he means that "Hegel seems to be in the impossible position of being both extraordinarily influential and almost completely inaccessible."[1] Any effort to provide access to that which is almost completely inaccessible is justified.

This book is on Hegel's *Science of Logic* (and not on any of Hegel's other works) because the *Logic*, more than the *Phenomenology of Spirit* or any of his other books, aims directly at the solution of what might be called *the* metaphysical problem, or, if one prefers, *the* ontological problem. The history of philosophy has taught us that a form of radical empiricism such as Hume's has disastrous consequences: It obliges us to commit to the flames concepts or words that are necessary for all language and thinking. Kant's critical philosophy saved them from the flames. In Kant's philosophy they were reinstated—*aufgehoben*, to use a non-Kantian, but key Hegelian concept—as categories. But Kant's philosophy ran into a *cul-de-sac*: His philosophy required the existence of an object (the thing in itself,

---

1. H. Sussman *The Hegelian Aftermath* (Baltimore and London: The Johns Hopkins University Press, 1982), here quoted from Robert Pippin *Hegel's Idealism: The Satisfaction of Self-Consciousness* (Cambridge: Cambridge University Press, 1989), 3.

das Ding an sich) of which one could say nothing[2]; none of the categories (i.e., none of the concepts constituting necessary conditions for experience and knowledge) could be applied to it, not even the category of existence. It was left to Absolute Idealism, inaugurated by Fichte and Schelling and completed by Hegel, to do away with the object as a thing in itself by transforming it into an object determined by the same categories as are thought and language. What Hegel said in the "Preface" to the *Phenomenology* is valid for all of his philosophy: "In my view, which can be justified only by the exposition of the system itself, everything turns on grasping and expressing the true, not only as substance, but equally as subject" (*PS* 10).

The aim of the *Logic* is to discover the categories—the categories that constitute the foundation of the subject as well as of the object, that is, the categories developed from a necessary beginning-point and by the logic of language—or if one prefers, by the necessity of thought—through all the intermediate categories to the final and all-embracing absolute idea. The absolute idea is precisely the category according to which object and subject achieve identity. Hegel's categories thus determine, or better, constitute both object and subject, both being and thought.

Hegel's *Science of Logic* is by almost universal consent regarded as his most difficult work, although it may also be his most important work; indeed, it may be the most important work on metaphysics in the history of philosophy. A work such as Hegel's *Science of Logic*, which aims to reveal the very foundation of all thinking and all ontology, neither can nor ought to be neglected by *Homo sapiens*.

To say that the aim of the *Logic* is to describe or to discover the categories—to describe or to discover the characteristics or properties of reason—could be misleading. It might suggest that the *Logic* is an inquiry that ultimately reveals how in fact reason is structured, though it is a contingent fact that reason is so structured. This is a misconception. Reason could under no circumstances be different from what it is. The categories by which reason is described, or better, is determined, are by necessity the same in all possible worlds. Reason is therefore not a psychological concept; if it were, it would be contingent. And because reason is what it is by necessity, it follows that metaphysics—as a function of reason—is what it is by necessity: There can be only one true metaphysics.

---

2. Cf. Friedrich Heinrich Jacobi's statement about *das Ding an sich*: "Without that assumption I could not enter the system, and with it I could not remain in it," *Kant: Philosophical Correspondence 1759–1799*, ed. and trans. Arnulf Zweig (Chicago: University of Chicago Press, 1967), 229.

If Hegel says that a great man condemns people to explicate his work, it can equally be said that the fact that man possesses reason commits him to a search for truth—the truth—the truth of metaphysics. A final reason to study Hegel's *Logic* is this: The fact that man is capable of metaphysical thought—i.e., is capable of a thinking that aims at the ultimate foundation of thought and being—commits him to a search for the truth of metaphysics.

A popular but false view is that the philosophical system—the metaphysics—of a country depends on the cultural view of that country. The truth is rather the opposite: the philosophical truth—the true metaphysics—determines the culture of a country—its art, its soul. In the "Preface" to the first edition of his *Science of Logic,* Hegel mentions "the strange spectacle of a cultured nation without metaphysics—like a temple richly ornamented in other respects but without a holy of holies" (*SL* 25).

Introduction

With Hegel, so-called 'Absolute Idealism' reached its culmination and its completion. This philosophy developed in order to correct what it took to be the fundamental errors of previous philosophies—especially to correct Kantianism, that is, to cure it from the conceptual blunders that led to the absurdity of the thing in itself.

I shall not here go into how Fichte replaced Kant's thing in itself with the universal or infinite ego, or how Schelling and Hegel replaced Fichte's universal or infinite ego with universal reason or the absolute.[3]

There is, however, an essential difference between Schelling's absolute and Hegel's absolute, namely: Schelling's absolute constitutes the foundation of all knowledge and cannot, therefore, itself be an object of knowledge. In Schelling's absolute, there is no difference between subject and object; there can be, therefore, no judgments and, consequently, no form of knowledge stated or expressed. In this respect, Hegel's absolute is just the opposite. Hegel criticizes Schelling's absolute by saying that it is "the night in which, as the saying goes, all cows are black" (*PS* 9).

Hegel's absolute does not constitute the foundation of all knowledge. Hegel's absolute is the truth of the system, and the truth of the system is not only the result obtained. It is the result understood as the result of the arguments and deductions (in Hegel's language, the dialectical movements of the concepts involved) leading up to it. In other words, the absolute is the total dialectical system, not just the result but also the steps leading up to it. Hegel illustrates the point in the following way: The blossom is preceded by the bud. When the bud bursts, the blossom comes out and, finally,

---

3. I have examined this development in detail in my book *From Radical Empiricism to Absolute Idealism*, Lewiston, New York: Mellen, 1986.

after the blossom comes the fruit. According to the view Hegel opposes, the bud, the blossom, and the fruit correspond to three mutually opposed philosophical systems, where at most only one can represent the truth, and the two others, if not all three, are false. Hegel contends that none of them is false. Each of them is a presupposition for the succeeding one. An essential part of what is meant by a bud is that it is a necessary and last step before the development of the blossom; it is what, by botanical necessity, precedes the existence of the blossom, just as what is meant by a fruit, at least in part, is what necessarily is preceded by the blossom (*PS* 2).[4]

Hegel's absolute is determined by the categories, the categories as they are specified dialectically in his *Logic*. In this respect and to this extent, there is a similarity between Kant and Hegel. But the difference between their concepts of a category is important; it illustrates and is an expression of the fundamental difference between Kantianism and Hegelianism.

The difference between the concept of a category in Kant's and in Hegel's philosophy is this: According to Kant a category is a concept constituting a condition of experience and knowledge. It is a concept the knowing subject applies to the so-called stuff of experience.

The idea that the categories are applied to this so-called stuff implies that this stuff exists independently of and prior to the categories. And because experience only occurs after the application of the categories, it follows that the stuff itself is logically excluded from being an object of experience and knowledge.

This conception of the category—that it is applied like an instrument—thus leads to a negation of knowledge. Because Hegel rejects the concept of the thing in itself, he accordingly must reject the instrument-theory of categories.[5]

Hegel's approach to categories is entirely different. In order to clarify Hegel's method, let me begin by restating what Hegel in his "Preface" to the *Phenomenology* proclaims as his aim: "In my view, which can be justified only by the exposition of the system itself, everything turns on

4. See also my *From Radical Empiricism to Absolute Idealism* (*op. cit.*), 93ff.

5. Hegel launches his criticism of Kant's instrument-theory in *Enz.* §10 and *Lectures on the History of Philosophy*, trans. E.S. Haldane and F.H. Simson, 3 vols. (New York: Humanities Press, 1955) III, 428. See also my essay "Categories and Things in Themselves," *Hegel's Critique of Kant*, ed. S. Priest (Oxford: Ashgate Publ. Co., 1987), 77–86.

grasping and expressing the true not only as substance but equally as subject" (*PS* 10).

In other words, substance, which here means the object as it is experienced in its supposed independent existence, is, according to common sense, a paradigm of individuality. Philosophical analysis, however, shows that the supposed individuality can be understood only in terms of universals.

Hegel's statement about his aim is consequently an important key to understanding his philosophy. As Herbert Marcuse puts it: ". . . the whole of the Hegelian system is a portrayal of the process whereby the individual becomes universal and whereby 'the construction of universality' takes place."[6]

How does this construction proceed? Hegel's beginning point was what could be called the commonsense world. That is the world as it is perceived by the senses; that is, it is a world in which objects are experienced to be at specific places at specific times. There are objects that can be reported to be here at this specific time, i.e., they are located as being 'here just now'. It is a world present on a pre-epistemological and a pre-metaphysical level. It is not a result of epistemological and metaphysical thinking; on the contrary, it is the point from which all epistemological and metaphysical thinking necessarily begins.[7] Hegel examines the world, and the language that describes it, in his chapter on "Sense-certainty" (*PS* 58–66). It can in many respects be compared to Plato's allegory of the cave as he describes it in *The Republic*. The prisoners, who are imprisoned in the cave, must necessarily believe what they directly experience. They are imprisoned by their epistemological and metaphysical ignorance, which does not mean that they have no beliefs; rather, instead of epistemological and metaphysical knowledge, they are possessed by false beliefs.

It is important to notice that in Plato's allegory, epistemological and metaphysical progress is achieved through the concept of negation. The aim of philosophical analysis is to negate—to falsify—the falsity of the beliefs held by the prisoners. This is important to notice because precisely by negating falsehoods Hegel progresses both in the *Phenomenology* and in the *Logic*.[8]

6. H. Marcuse *Reason and Revolution* (Oxford: Oxford University Press, 1941), 90.

7. Cf. P.F. Strawson *Individuals* (London: Methuen & Co. Ltd., 1959), 15f.

8. In the "Preface" to the *Phenomenology,* Hegel speaks of "the tremendous power of the negative; it is the energy of thought, of the pure 'I' " (*PS* 19).

What Hegel negates concerning our commonsense view and our commonsense language, that is, the language we use in order to talk about our commonsense world, is not our use of the words we in fact use. That would be to commit the fallacy committed by Hume, whose radical empiricism would commit to the flames all words which were not connected with sense impressions and would thus impoverish the language to the point that it could not be used as a language. Hegel would subscribe to what Wittgenstein proclaimed almost 150 years later, namely that language is in order as it is.[9] Hegel is not correcting our language—we shall still have to use words such as 'I', 'here', 'now', and 'this'. He corrects our *understanding* of these words. He negates the incorrect assumption that individual utterances of such words name individual particulars. Philosophical analysis reveals that these words can be used and understood only within a context of universals.[10] Our negating power takes us in the *Phenomenology* from one form of consciousness to another—it takes us from sense-certainty, through perception and force and understanding, to self-consciousness.

A so-called 'form of consciousness' is determined by the nature of the object—the object of consciousness. Two forms of consciousness differ if the objects constituting the objects of consciousness are different. There is, for example, a difference between a consciousness according to which objects are conceived as individual particulars and a consciousness according to which objects are conceived as universals. Of necessity, we are talking about objects, but the nature of the objects is conceived differently. We are therefore talking about two different forms of consciousness. The negating power—or, if one prefers, our capacity for philosophical analysis—enables us to see that one form of consciousness needs correction and, consequently, moves to the corrected one. This correction implies that the concept of the object is preserved, but the false concept of what an object is has now been replaced by the correct one. This way of philosophizing

9. L. Wittgenstein *Philosophical Investigations* (London: Macmillan, 1953), I §98 (p. 45).

10. Cf. G.E. Moore's statement in his essay "A Defence of Common Sense," concerning certain common sense propositions, for example "The Earth has existed for many years past." Some philosophers, he says, are confusing the question whether we understand its meaning (which we certainly do) with the entirely different question whether we know what it means, in the sense that we are able to give a correct analysis of its meaning. J.H. Muirhead, ed., *Contemporary British Philosophy* (Second Series; London: George Allen & Unwin Ltd., 1925), 198.

Hegel terms *zu aufheben*, which is usually translated into English as 'to sublate'.[11]

We thus see that according to Hegel we reach knowledge, not by applying categories as tools or, as he says, as spears and staves, but by finding out through philosophical analysis what must be negated and therefore eliminated and what must be preserved (*sublated*).[12] Hegel's categories are consequently not tools, they are not spears and staves; instead, they identify the object of absolute knowledge; they identify the absolute.

Another and fundamental difference between Kant's and Hegel's categories is this: Kant's categories are the subject's tools with which it attacks the object. They are therefore, in a sense, subjective.[13] The categories in Kant's philosophy categorize the object, that is, they make the object appear in such a way that it can be an object of experience. However, as an object of experience, it differs from the object in itself—an object that by definition cannot be known.

In Hegel's philosophy, the categories constitute and define the absolute. In the absolute, we learn, the true is grasped and expressed "not only as substance but equally as subject." This implies that the categories constitute, they are valid of and identify, subject and substance equally. In other words, the object in itself is not unknown; it is known because it is an object that is constituted by the categories. The categories identify, describe, and constitute both subject and substance. Hegel's categories are consequently ontological categories. They are categories not only for all thought, but also categories for the world. This is why a main thesis in Hegel's philosophy is that being and thought are identical.

In the "Preface" to the second edition of the *Science of Logic* Hegel writes: "The forms of thought are, in the first instance, displayed and

---

11. On forms of consciousness and Hegel's phenomenological dialectic, see K.R. Westphal, "Hegel's Solution to the Dilemma of the Criterion," in *The Phenomenology of Spirit Reader: A Collection of Critical and Interpretive Essays*, J. Stewart, ed. (Albany: State University of New York Press, 1998), 76–91.

12. Hegel's point is that the verb *zu aufheben* has a double meaning; it means partly to annihilate and partly to preserve—in the sense that in its preserved form it is purified from the false conception.

13. See note 5. Only in a sense, because the subject is not the empirical and individual subject; it is the universal subject, which is a descendant of Kant's transcendental apperception; transcendental apperception constitutes the logical conditions for the categories. Cf. Werner Marx, *Hegel's Phenomenology of Spirit* (New York: Harper & Row, 1975), 17.

stored in human language. Nowadays we cannot be reminded too often that thinking <u>distinguishes man from beast</u>" (*SL* 31). Or, expressed differently, *it is through a study of the logical structure of language that the categories are revealed or discovered.* It is also, therefore, through such a study that the categories of the world are revealed or discovered. This accords with Hegel's dictum that there is identity between thought and being, or, in other words, that the categories are ontologically valid.

This identity can be illustrated as follows: Language is about something. It seems at first trivially true to say that language is about a nonlinguistic reality. Admittedly, language can be about language. I can use language to speak about another language, which in turn might be designed to speak about yet another language, and so forth. But in order to avoid obvious logical difficulties, it must be the case that there is a language that is not about another language but about a nonlinguistic reality.

It is important, however, to distinguish between (1) the fact stated, (2) the stating of the fact, and (3) that which makes the stating true or false.[14] That is, that which I state or say something about belongs to the fact category. I state, assert, or say something about an object; I state or assert a fact about an object. About the cat I can say that it is on the mat, about the window that it is open, etc. Obviously, I can say something about an object, but I cannot *say* an object. What makes the stating true or false is the fact stated. If the cat is in fact on the mat, or the window is in fact open, then the statement that the cat is on the mat or that the window is open is true; otherwise, it is false. The important thing to notice is this: <u>The fact that makes the statement true or false is nonlinguistic reality.</u> But this nonlinguistic reality is, as mentioned, itself a fact (it is a fact that the cat is on the mat or that the window is open). <u>This means that it displays the appropriate concepts</u> (namely, in these cases, the concepts 'cat', 'mat', 'window', and 'open', among others). <u>A fact is a fact precisely because it displays the concepts in question; it displays them—they are involved. And because concepts entail language, it follows that the nonlinguistic reality, which language is about, is after all also itself a linguistic reality.</u> This is true insofar as <u>nonlinguistic reality can be in consciousness</u> or be given meaning only as <u>conceptualized.</u>

We cannot say that a fact itself is an unconceptualized stuff, and be-

---

14. For detailed analyses of the relation between the stating of a fact and the fact stated, see my "Language and its Object," *Philosophy and Phenomenological Research* 38 (1977–78), 239–246, and "An Essay in Ontology," *Revue Internationale de Philosophie* 135 (1981), 60–73.

comes a fact only after concepts are applied to it. If we could, the 'it' to which the concepts are supposedly applied would then itself be a nothing. To say that something is unconceptualized contravenes the meaning of the concept 'something'. Nothing can be anything unless it is conceptualized. Concepts constitute the necessary conditions for the existence of facts. They constitute facts; they are part and parcel of facts.

In other words, the stating of the facts and the facts stated are, in the sense just described, identical.

With What Must the Science of Logic Begin?

The Logic's plot: the failure of immediacy

scientifically = immediacy?

The Concepts of the Mediated and the Immediate

Two concepts—the concept of the mediated and the concept of the immediate—play an important role in Hegel's logic. We meet them already in Hegel's first question, namely, whether the beginning of the logical system is mediated or immediate. The term 'science' could be misleading. Hegel asks whether our investigation of the very foundation of all thinking, that is, our investigation of the system of categories, has certain presuppositions from which it is derived; in that case the beginning would be *autonomous* mediated. If it is not so derived, then its beginning is immediate. However we answer, we face a problem. If the beginning is mediated, the truth of the categorical system depends upon the truth of that from which it is derived. An infinite regress thus seems unavoidable. If instead the beginning is immediate, it is impossible to give any arguments or reasons for its truth. In this case, it will be impossible to decide between different competing systems. Or rather, because there can be no criterion of the truth of the system, the question of its truth cannot be asked. This is unacceptable. It is unacceptable because what we are aiming at is *the* system. There can be one and only one system of categories. There can be only one foundation on which all our knowledge and all our thinking rests, one and only one categorical system that is displayed in our language and that makes being the being it is by necessity.

Hegel's answer to this problem is that it is a false dichotomy. As he puts it: "There is nothing, nothing in heaven or in nature or mind or anywhere else which does not equally contain both immediacy and mediation, so that these determinations reveal themselves to be *unseparated* and inseparable and the opposition between them to be null" (*SL* 68).

In other words, the beginning of logic is both mediated and immediate. It is mediated because logic presupposes phenomenology. It presupposes the result that the true is grasped and expressed "not only as substance but equally as subject." As mentioned in the introduction, Hegel arrives at this result through a philosophical analysis of the different forms of consciousness (beginning with our commonsense view), which are sublated through the method of determinate negation. What we finally arrive at is that, although our commonsense language (and view) is unchallenged, our conception of the 'object', the 'here', the 'now', and the 'I' have been refined or have been deepened. We now understand that what we mistakenly thought were concrete individuals enjoying independent existence are in fact universals. We understand, to quote Marcuse again, that: "The whole of the Hegelian system is a portrait of the process whereby the individual becomes universal and whereby the construction of universality takes place."

According to the *Phenomenology*, Cartesian dualism is false: We do not have two qualitatively different substances, extended substance (*res extensa*) and thinking substance (*res cogitans*), but just one substance, namely, a substance that (because it is constituted by universals) is also a universal subject. The *Phenomenology* does not, however, map out the logical structure of, or lay bare the logical connection among, the categories of the universal subject. Precisely because it is necessary, this logical structure is universally valid. To find the logical tie between the categories—to describe the logical system of the categories—is the aim of the *Logic*.

In understanding this task, the *Logic* is mediated (it presupposes the result of the *Phenomenology*); but its beginning is also immediate because the task of laying out the categories and their logical connections presupposes nothing but thought itself.

However, only with some qualification is Hegel right in stating "that there is nothing in heaven or in nature or in mind or anywhere else which does not equally contain both immediacy and mediation." As mentioned, the *Phenomenology* began with our commonsense view, expressed by commonsense (or ordinary) language; but such a beginning can hardly be called mediated, for it is not a result of reflection, nor is it deduced from anything. It constitutes the necessary condition for all consciousness and language. It satisfies such necessary conditions—as P.F. Strawson made abundantly clear—as having identifiable and reidentifiable objects.[15] Kant would say that these conditions are satisfied because our categories impose those conditions on the stuff (he would commit what could be called the

15. Strawson, *Individuals* (*op. cit.*), 15–58.

Kantian fallacy), whereas Hegel, who identifies being and thought (substance and subject), would say that substance as well as subject express, they are constituted by, they are even (in a sense) created by, the categories.

It is one thing, however, to clarify the beginning of logic in terms of the concepts of immediacy and mediation, in particular, to clarify in what sense the beginning may be said to be immediate. It is another thing to determine which category necessarily must begin logic—to determine which category is the first category of logic.

Hegel's *Logic* is a determination of categories, the categories that are categories of both thought and being. They are concepts, therefore, that are not—could not be—derived empirically. They could not be derived empirically because the empirical world is what it is due to the categories; they constitute the conditions of the empirical world. The beginning point cannot, therefore, be an empirical datum; it must be a pure thought determination, that is, a concept without any empirical element. Because it is the first category, that is, the category that follows from nothing but itself, it is a presupposition of all other categories. In short, it must be empirically empty and conceptually nonderivable. The only concept that satisfies these conditions is the concept of pure being.

Being

[handwritten: Lemma begins T + O The of same way!]

Pure Being and Nothing

[handwritten: i.e. "logically" Being is not 1st?]

Beginning a logical system with the concept of pure being poses difficult philosophical problems. The logic of the verb 'to be' requires that there is something of which it can be said that it is—that it has being, and that this 'something' is characterized by its properties. To be is to be something. To simplify Bertrand Russell's point: To assert about something that it exists, is to assert that there is at least one x such that this x has a certain property.[16] *[handwritten: construing 'nothing' as the peculiar]*

By definition, pure being is precisely that which is nothing. It is a being that has no properties; it is a being from which all properties have been abstracted, or rather a being to which no properties have been ascribed. It is a 'being', therefore, that does not satisfy the logical conditions for being called 'being''. *[handwritten: The Being "is" not.]*

Thus it is obvious that if the concept of pure being is meant as an ontological concept, then that concept is a logical failure. It is a concept whose creation results from overstepping—transcending—the logical conditions for such a concept. The concept of pure being cannot serve as an ontological concept.

Hegel expresses the conceptual fact that the concept of pure being is ontologically empty by saying that it is identical with the concept of nothing. In other words, from the concept of pure being the concept of nothing follows. The two concepts are identical insofar as they both are ontologically empty. *[handwritten: No - The 2nd "is" The emphasis]*

---

16. B. Russell "The Philosophy of Logical Atomism," *The Monist* (1918–19), reprinted in *Bertrand Russell: Logic and Knowledge*, ed. Robert C. Marsh (London: George Allen & Unwin Ltd., 1956), 175–281. *[handwritten: of The 1st.]*

11

It may be objected that if the concept of pure being is regarded as an ontological concept and is thus a logical miscarriage—a concept that has collapsed—nothing can follow from it; a collapsed concept, a misconstrued concept, cannot be a member of the logical language game) Although this concept is ontologically empty or, better, cannot be used as an ontological concept, it does not follow that the concept has no sense. If it were a nonsensical concept, we could not assert that the concept was a nonontological concept. In fact, as has been emphasized by Gottlob Frege, concepts have partly an ontological dimension or function and partly an analytical function. Frege does not use these terms. He speaks of 'meaning' and 'sense'; I shall use the terms 'denotation' and 'connotation'.[17] The term 'denotation' refers to that which the term names, stands for, refers to, or picks out. The statement, (1) "The morning star is a body illuminated by the Sun," refers to the planet Venus. The denotation of the statement is thus the planet Venus. Consider next the statement, (2) "The evening star is a body illuminated by the Sun." This statement happens to refer to the same planet, namely Venus. In other words, (1) and (2) have the same denotation. Nevertheless, (1) and (2) are different statements insofar as the expression 'evening star' differs from the expression 'morning star'. These two expressions have different connotations. As Frege writes: "Anybody who did not know that the evening star is the morning star might hold the one thought to be true, the other false."[18]

That expressions may connote despite the fact that they do not denote is obvious. To take another of Frege's examples: The statement, "The celestial body most distant from the Earth," has very clear connotations but may not have any denotation. (Within a room, we can talk about the chair most distant from me; within a country, the town most distant from me; but if we talk about the universe, it is of course quite another matter.)[19]

---

17. G. Frege "Sinn und Bedeutung," *Zeitschrift für Philosophie und philosophische Kritik* 100 (1892), 25–50; translated in *Translations from the Philosophical Writings of Gottlob Frege*, eds. P. Geach and M. Black (Oxford: Blackwell, 1952), 56–78. For present purposes, I shall use the older terms 'denotation' and 'connotation' for '*Bedeutung*' and '*Sinn*', respectively, and leave aside problems regarding the exact interpretation and proper translation from German into English of these Fregean terms.

18. *Ibid.*, 62.

19. *Ibid.*, 58.

To return to the concepts of pure being and nothing, these concepts both have connotations but no denotation.[20] On analysis, what we mean by the concept of pure being is most definitely different from what we mean by the concept of nothing. From the analysis of the concept of pure being *follows* its ontological emptiness. From the concept of nothing, its ontological emptiness does not follow; it is *expressed*. To illustrate the logical difference between the concept 'follow from' and the concept 'directly express', imagine that we have a box that contains only twenty items. Then imagine that these twenty items are removed. Accordingly, we may make the following true statements: (a) "From this box we have removed all twenty items it contained," and (b) "This box is empty." Statements (a) and (b) have the same denotation. But they do not have the same connotations. From (a) I infer that the box is empty, but this I do not *infer* from (b); (b) states it directly.

Findlay, who wrote the foreword to Wallace's translation of Hegel's *Encyclopaedia*, says this: "The doctrine of being begins with the much too famous triad of being, nothing and becoming, which does no more than attest the indistinguishable emptiness of categories which are without the internal differentiation of mutually contrasted definites or finites. Hegel's philosophy is a philosophy of the definite, the finite, almost from the start: it can attach no meaning to notions in which all fades out in an Oriental blur."[21] Findlay can pass this judgment only because he does not distinguish (as little as do other commentators or even Hegel himself) between the denotation and the connotation of the concept of pure being.

---

20. In the chapter, "The Lion and the Unicorn," of Lewis Carroll's *Through the Looking Glass,* we have a case of what happens when a word without denotation but with clear connotations nevertheless is used as if it was an ontological word. The King asks Alice if she can see either of the two messengers sent out: "Just look along the road, and tell me if you can see either of them." "I see nobody on the road," said Alice. "I only wish I had such eyes," the King remarked in a fretful tone. "To be able to see nobody! And at that distance too! Why, it is as much as I can see real people by the light."

21. *Hegel's Logic*, trans. W. Wallace (Oxford: Clarendon Press, 1975), xviii. Among the many philosophers who have not understood Hegel is also John Stuart Mill. This is demonstrated in a conversation he had with the Danish critic George Brandes. In this conversation, Mill declares that Hegel's logic is nonsense. To begin the *Logic* by identifying being and nothing seems to Mill to be a proof of the nonsensicalness of Hegel's logic and metaphysics. Had Mill used his own distinction between denotation and connotation, he would have seen the incorrectness of his criticism. Cf. Brandes *Samlede værker* (Collected Works) IX, 540f.

[handwritten top margin: Does this imply that logic's most difficult move, its reconciliation of the severest antithesis, is its very move? Is this difficulty a function of the fact that the Logic begins with the simplest determination?]

That Hegel does not keep this distinction clearly in mind can be seen from what he says in the *Encyclopaedia*. "In *representation*, or for the understanding, the proposition: '*Being and nothing is the same*', appears to be such a paradoxical proposition that it may perhaps be taken as not seriously meant. And it really is one of the hardest propositions that thinking dares to formulate, for being and nothing are the antithesis in all its *immediacy*" (*Enz.* §88). The paradoxical aspect disappears when it is seen that the two concepts are *not* identical in connotation, even though they are identical in denotation. Their difference in connotation is shown by the logical fact that from the concept of pure being follows its ontological emptiness, whereas the concept of nothing directly expresses its ontological emptiness.

[handwritten left margin: Does this shed light on Hegel's way of understanding the Logic?]

The Concept of Becoming

Besides the concept of pure being and the concept of nothing, Hegel introduces a third concept: the concept of becoming. This concept is supposed to connect the concepts of pure being and nothing. This concept, Hegel maintains, unites those two concepts. What does it mean—what *could* it mean—to say that the concept of pure being *becomes* the concept of pure nothing? *[handwritten: (1)]* Because the primary function of the concept of becoming is to refer to a process through which something is created, it seems highly inappropriate to use it in connection with logical relations. This is why Hegel has been accused of bringing movement into logic.[22] This accusation is entirely unjustified. The fact that the concept of becoming, conceived as a process, requires the concept 'something', namely the something that becomes (or changes), excludes the ontologically empty concept of pure being. Becoming as a process can be used only in the context of what Hegel calls determinate being (*Dasein*).[23] *[handwritten: Rather Becoming is the Truth of Becoming where it is actual.]*

[handwritten left margin: it, an wonder??]

---

22. Trendelenburg, and after him Kierkegaard, criticized Hegel for, as they expressed it, bringing movement into logic.

23. Kuno Fischer suggests that the best way to view the transition from becoming to determinate being is to refer to the concept of time. Time is precisely a Heraclitean flow. Consequently, determinate being exists only in the time which has already passed. About determinate being, Fischer says: "thus it can only be grasped as a past process, as a vanished vanishing, as a past becoming or having become, i.e. determinate being (*Dasein*)" (*Hegels Leben, Werken und Lehre* [Heidelberg: Carl Winters Universitätsbuchhandlung, 1911] I, 51). Such a view is obviously untenable: The time which has passed is not pure time, but a time in which something has happened; in other words a time belonging to determinate being. The nontem-

[handwritten bottom: (1) This is precisely what Hegel does not say: between Nothing and Being is only an Übergegangenheit, not an Übergehen.]

In what sense can we say that the concept of becoming connects or unites the concepts of pure being and nothing? One of the difficulties with Hegel's analysis of the concept of becoming is that his language suggests that he deals, not with pure being, but with being (that is, determinate being). If we are dealing with being (and not with pure being), there is no difficulty because we are then dealing with a 'something' that is changing from something into something else. But if we are dealing with pure being, there is no 'something' and consequently no 'something else' and therefore no change. Pure being does not change into nothing, nor does nothing change into pure being. In what sense, if any, does the concept of becoming find a place in the context of pure being? The place it may find implies that the concept of becoming takes on a sense that deviates from ordinary language (it therefore misled, among others, Trendelenburg and Kierkegaard). We may say that when we understand the connotation of pure being we understand that it is (that it 'becomes') ontologically empty; that is, it is identical with (it 'becomes') the concept of nothing. Or we may say: From the connotation of the concept of pure being its denotation is derived, that is, we derive its ontological emptiness, we derive the concept of nothing. Or instead of using the concept of derivation we may without misleading use the concept of becoming. Instead of saying: From the concept of pure being we derive the concept of nothing, we may say: Pure being becomes nothing. Just as the concept of derivation (implication, entailment, etc.) connects or unites that from which something is implied with the implied, so the logical use of 'becoming' connects or unites that which is becoming with that which it becomes (in the present example, pure being becomes nothing). What we have seen so far is that logic must begin with the concept of pure being. To restate the argument as briefly as possible: Because the *Logic* "is to be understood as the system of pure reason as the realm of pure thought," or as Hegel also states, "the system of logic is the realm of shadows, the world of simple essentialities freed from all sensuous concreteness" (*SL* 50, 58), it follows that the *Logic* cannot begin with anything that already is a something (a 'something' already contains categories). Consequently, the beginning must be a being without a determination, that is, the beginning must be a pure being.

poral character of Hegel's logic is stressed by Th. Wartenberg, "Hegel's Idealism: The Logic of Conceptuality," in *The Cambridge Companion to Hegel*, F.C. Beiser, ed. (Cambridge: Cambridge University Press, 1993), 102–129.

The Concept of Determinate Being and the Concept of Negation

The transition from pure being to determinate being is characterized by the fact that pure being, which is (becomes) nothing, changes into determinate being, a being that becomes a something. Through this transition, the concept of nothing changes into (becomes) a negating power: Determinate being is a something. As a something, it necessarily negates all that which it is not; it is both something and a negation of other things. The determining feature of, for example, a triangle—its definition—is understood only by understanding what it excludes[24]; it excludes features that define all other geometrical figures, such as a circle and a square. To speak with Hegel, it can be said that a thing is that which it is not, by which he means, the identity conditions of any one thing are determined by their negating—excluding—the identity conditions of other things. If we call the definition of a triangle 'T' and all the qualities that are not features of a triangle 'non-T', we may say that a triangle is both T and non-T; because the concept of non-T is built into the concept of T, the two concepts are inseparable. This point also holds for the causal characteristics of anything; those characteristics are essential to what something is (to its identity conditions), and those characteristics necessarily relate to the causal characteristics (and hence to the identity conditions) of other things.

This language better suits "Essence" than "Being"

It is interesting to see how contradiction finds its necessary place in Hegelian philosophy. The necessity of the negation is as true (is as necessary) as it is true (of necessity) that any determinate being must possess not only its specific (positive) qualities, but also the corresponding negative qualities. It must possess the qualities that negate the positive qualities. To understand the connotation of 'something', it is necessary to understand the negative qualities that constitute the negation of the positive qualities possessed by that 'something'. The concept of nothing (the denotation of pure being) is in determinate being transformed into a negating function; that is, it negates the 'something' of determinate being. In other words, the concept of nothing—the denotation of pure being—is an ineradicable

So from the beginning the principle of contradiction is ontological not merely logical, even in this purely logical context

---

24. This is the Spinozistic principle accepted by Hegel (*SL* 113) as fundamental: "Determination is negation posited as affirmative" and is the proposition by Spinoza: "*omnis determinatio est negatio*" (Espistola 50). E.E. Harris maintains that this formulation is nowhere to be found in the works of Spinoza, *An Interpretation of the Logic of Hegel* (Lanham: University Press of America, 1983), 122.

I think you're ahead [of yourself] — here there is determinate being, but not yet a force determining. That will require the [?]

element of the concept of being—of pure as well as of determinate being. In determinate being, it becomes a negating force. The less content something has, the more is negated. If something vanishes, then the negating force becomes identical with nothing — and the determinate being will be identical with pure being. *of determinate being with becoming.*

Hegel's dependence on Heraclitus is well-known. In his *Logic,* he describes Heraclitus as deep-thinking and praises him for having brought forward the higher, total concept of *becoming (SL* 83); and in his *History of Philosophy,* Hegel writes: "With Heraclitus we see land; there is no proposition of Heraclitus which I have not adopted in my *Logic.*"[25] ①

The becoming Heraclitus talks about is a concept of the structure of the world. It is not a logical concept in the sense in which Hegel's concept of becoming is of a logical nature when he investigates the relation between pure being and nothing. Heraclitus' concept of becoming belongs to the world of objects. Within this world, according to Heraclitus, there is a constant flux. The world is conceived as being in a constant coming-to-be and ceasing-to-be. At each moment, there is something that comes-to-be that nevertheless at that very same moment ceases-to-be. (If this were not so, there would be a moment, however short, where there was something that did not change.) The result is by necessity that there isn't anything at any moment: It is either about to be, that is, it cannot yet be said to be, it *is* not; or it has already been, it already has ceased to be and therefore *is* not. Thus the Heraclitean world as constant flux leads by necessity to a collapse of the concept of a world. It is a self-destructive world.

At the same time, however, because Hegel not only accepts the concept of becoming—in fact, not only accepts but regards it as a most important one—he does not apply it to the world of objects. For Hegel, this concept is applicable to the behavior of the categories. It presupposes that we have moved into the conceptual realm of determinate being. That is, we have moved into the realm of concepts which, due to the concept of negation, the categories have determined as a something as well as a something else. Because of the concept of negation, one category *becomes* another category, and in this other category (the category that has become), the former category, or rather the true part of it, is preserved, is sublated. Because the concept of becoming means the logical movement of the categories, it obviously cannot be understood as a physical movement or a time-process.

① In [?] (?) to SL he says this of Plato's [?] ⎱ Parmenides

---

25. *Lectures on the History of Philosophy,* op. cit., I, 279.

It was stressed earlier that, within the context of pure being and nothing, the concept of becoming was to be understood as 'implying' or 'entailing', and consequently could no more be understood as a time-process than could the statement that the sum of the angles in a triangle becomes 180°. Analogously, it can be said that the logical movement of one category to another (or, if one prefers, the movement through which one category becomes another category) is only absurdly regarded as a time-process. Therefore, to say (as Trendelenburg and Kierkegaard did) that Hegel brought movements (movement as a time-process) into logic is not to have understood Hegel. The development, the movement, or the becoming of the categorical system results from the negation built into every concept. No concept is only what it is; it is also, as we have just seen, and just as much, that which it is not. It is no trivial matter to say, for example, that brown as such includes all the colors that are different from brown. Brown gets its brownness precisely because it is none of the other colors—because it excludes them. If everything in the world was brown, the word 'brown' would be meaningless.

The preceding treatment of the concept of becoming has only, to a small degree, been an interpretation; it has, however, to a greater degree, been an attempt at clarification. The reason a clarification seems to be needed is this: Hegel's language sometimes suggests that, like Heraclitus, he thinks of becoming as a time-process; that is, it suggests that he would be engaged in an investigation that ultimately would be empirical. But Hegel's investigation is obviously a logical or conceptual investigation. It is an investigation into the categories, their existence, and their logical relations; it is therefore an investigation that is entirely different from any empirical investigation.

That the concept of becoming understood as a time-process is a conceptual absurdity does not mean, of course, that the concept itself is a logical miscarriage. We often use the concept, and often with good sense, in contexts where we talk about a process; we say such things as: I am about to become sick; I become older as time goes by; as the child attends school, she or he becomes more and more educated. It is when we talk about becoming as a process, as something that occurs between nothing and the resulting being, that we are misled. Suppose that I have mislaid something and am looking for it. Suddenly I find it. As everybody knows, it would be absurd to speak about a certain 'finding process', i.e., a process during which I could be said neither to have not found it nor to have found it—a process that takes place in a sort of no-man's land. By its very logic, the verb 'to find' can be classified among what Gilbert Ryle called achievement verbs.[26] It is the kind of verb that implies that the moment the present tense applies so does the past tense: Whenever I say "Now I find it," I also could have said "I found it." Other such verbs are perception verbs: to see is to have seen, to hear is to have heard, and the like. Wittgenstein's analysis of the expression "Now I understand" amounts to very much the same thing: The moment I can say "Now I understand" I have already understood.

ooh. oh, an ideational 'reading' of the Logos

---

26. Cf. my *History of Philosophy* (Odense: Odense University Press; New York: Humanities, 1976), 9; and "Movement, Moments, and Beginning," *Theoria* 30 (1964), 75–79.

Quality

Becoming and Determinate Being

Something and Something Else

To summarize the logical steps taken so far: The beginning point, that is, the necessary presupposition, is our commonsense view: the world of identifiable and reidentifiable objects. We all understand the meaning of statements involving such objects (commonsense statements). But, like Moore, we may say that there is a difference between understanding the meaning of such commonsense statements and knowing the correct analysis of the meaning of such statements. From the commonsense point of view, we move to pure being, that is, the concept of uncategorized being, the concept the denotation of which is nothing. In order to get a concept of being that has a denotation, we must apply the Spinozistic principle: We must determine by negating. In doing so, we get a concept of being that is something. We now locate a being that is distinct from something else. In other words, to talk about a 'something' is to imply a 'something else'. What this implies, furthermore, is that no 'something' can ever, so to speak, stand alone; its identity conditions must include the identity conditions of that which it is not. For example, to say something is yellow means (and it would have no meaning if it could not be said) that it is neither blue, black, brown, white, nor red, and so on. However detailed a description I give of the properties of a thing—the properties without which the thing in question would not be this specific thing—that description would be incomprehensible if the negation of these properties were not understood. If I say about butter that it is yellow, soft, and edible, it would be incompre-

20

But this manner of reading Hegel makes 'dialectic' internal to "saying" – it makes logic merely logical — *Hegel's "logic":*

hensible if I did not know what it would mean to say that yellow is a color that contrasts with all the other colors, such as red, green, blue, and so on, or to say that softness is that which contrasts, for example, with hardness and fluidity. To say about something that its defining property is, say, A, and A contrasts with B, C, and D, is to say that A gets its meaning by being non-B, non-C, and non-D. A is the positive value, whereas B, C, and D are the negative values (with respect to A). — *I.e., this reading imposes a "contextual" as Kantian goal.*

Obviously, the concepts of something and of something else are categories. They are necessary concepts to get from pure being to determinate being. About pure being, it is logically excluded to ask what it is. The concept of 'what' cannot apply to pure being. Determinate being, however, would not be determinate being if there were no answer to the question of its whatness. The minimum answer is noninformative: It is something. The concept of something, and therefore also the concept of something else, are consequently not only categories of determinate being, but they are also its first categories, that is, first in the logical sense. Because they are categories of thought, they are consequently also categories of language. It would be impossible to have a language without the concept of 'something' and therefore also without the concept of 'something else'.

Bad Infinity

The concept of 'something' implies by necessity the concept of 'something else'. The two concepts limit each other. But just as the 'something' by necessity implies the 'something else', so the concept of 'something else' in itself is a 'something'. That is, it is a 'something else' only insofar as it is that which limits the 'something'. In itself the 'something else' is a 'something', and as a 'something' it, as we have just seen, entails a 'something else', and because the new 'something else' itself is a 'something', it also is a 'something else'. And so on infinitely. Such an infinity Hegel calls the bad infinity (*die schlechte Unendlichkeit*).

The reason Hegel characterizes it as bad is this: It is an endless series of finite items, that is, of items that, by necessity, are finite and also, by necessity, must continue to the next item. From the very fact that its continuation is logically built into it, it follows that there is a conflict between what the series requires, namely, its continuation to completion, and the logical impossibility of such a completion. It is part of the meaning of the

concept of 'incomplete' that what is incomplete should be complete. That
is, the concept 'incomplete' implies an ought—an ought to complete the
incomplete.[27]

True Infinity

True infinity is not, in contrast to bad infinity, a series that continues
infinitely—continues infinitely in the same way as, for example, a straight
line may be continued infinitely. True infinity is comparable to a circle. It is
an infinity where a something implies a something else; this something
else, in turn, is seen to imply that very something by which it was implied.
In order to see that this is so, it is necessary once more to examine the concept, all important for Hegel's philosophy, of negation. Each 'something'
has (to reiterate) positive value and corresponding negative values. This
involves each 'something' being not only that which it is, but also that
which it is not. If a 'something' is, say, 'A' then to be 'A' means to be that
which is not 'non-A'. However, if 'A' is 'something', then that which is
'non-A' must be 'something else'. Therefore 'something' is both 'A' and
that which is not 'non-A'; and because not 'non-A' is 'something else', it
follows that 'something' is identical with 'something else': Their identity
conditions are interdefined.

It is important to note that when we speak about 'A' and 'non-A', then
the class of 'non-A' includes whatever belongs to the same class of things as
'A' does. To go back to the example of colors, if 'A' is red, then 'non-A' is the
class of all other colors. And, obviously, 'A' is only red insofar as it cannot

27. "This *infinity* is *spurious or negative* infinity, since it is nothing but the negation of the finite, but the finite arises again in the same way, so that it is no more
sublated than not. In other words, this infinity expresses only the requirement that
the finite *ought* to be sublated. This process ad infinitum does not go beyond the
expression of the contradiction, which the finite contains, [i.e.,] that it is just as
much *something* as its *other*, and [this process] is the perpetual continuation of the
alternation between these determinations, each bringing in the other one" (*Enz.*
§94). In the *Logic,* Hegel expresses it thus: "This spurious infinity is in itself the
same thing as the perennial ought; it is the negation of the finite it is true, but it cannot in truth free itself therefrom. The finite re-appears in the infinite itself as its
other, because it is only in its connection with its other, the finite, that the infinite
is. The progress to infinity is, consequently, only the perpetual repetition of one
and the same content, one and the same tedious alternation of this finite and infinite" (*SL* 142).

But is this 'physical' example an example of the 'logical' in your narrow, subjective sense?

be said to be any other color. To say that it is red is to say that the color it is, is none of the other colors. If red was the only color, there could be no color whatever. In order to be a color at all, any color requires other colors with which it contrasts; if there were no such other colors, no color name could have any meaning. To say that a thing is that which it is not is thus a proposition whose truth is required as well from an ontological point of view as from a logical point of view.

Key

The true infinity has absorbed the finite. In themselves, the 'something' and the 'something else' are finite, and as long as their identity is not understood, they constitute elements of bad infinity; but if their identity is understood, it is understood that it is a negation of the negation—understood that it is a self-negation and therefore a self-limitation—then it is understood that they constitute elements of true infinity.

True Infinity

It might be misleading to speak about the 'something' and the 'something else' as if we were speaking about two things or two ontological entities instead of just one thing; and that one thing can, however, be conceived as a something as well as a something else. The movement from something to something else is, of course, a conceptual movement. The assumption that it should be a physical movement (*pace* Trendelenburg and Kierkegaard) can hardly be given any sense.

→ a statement that diminishes Hegel's Phil of Nature. There is "logical" movement in Hegel's Logic! the controlled equivocation of H's dialectic.

Being-for-Self

→ the

True infinity is a category. It is a category because it applies by necessity to whatever is. There is nothing which is not identical with that which negates it; their identity conditions are interdefined. Or, to express it differently, everything is that which it is not.

This statement seems flatly to contradict Bishop Butler's oft-quoted statement that a thing is what it is and not another thing. This merely appears to be a contradiction. To Hegel, as well as to Butler, as well as to anybody else, a house is a house (and not a tree) and a cow is a cow (and not a horse) and the number two is number two (and not number three). And if Butler could have read Hegel, he would have agreed with him, namely that nothing could be anything but nothing if it was not determined by the negative properties. Hegel's statement would be less provocative, however, if it were expressed by stating the claim that to possess a property P is to possess the properties that negate non-P. P can only be P if there are properties belonging to the same class of properties as P, but that differ from P. If this is not the case, P could no longer be called a property.

What about the series of natural numbers? This series is taken to be not only a prototype of bad infinity but also as a series that, it is claimed, cannot be conceived as a true infinity. How, for instance, can the number two be identical with that which it is not—identical with, say, the number three? This, obviously, it cannot be. The number two is, most definitely, not identical with the number three. However, the number two would be nothing if there were no numbers one, three, or four. The number two is what it is because it is the number between one and three. That is, it is number two precisely because it is neither number one nor number three. We could express it this way: The number two has the negative properties of being neither number one nor number three. These negative properties define the number two. The number two is thus a negation of its negation.

Closely connected with the category of true infinity is the category of being-for-self. True infinity concerns (at least) two finite elements—the something and the something else—regarding which, as soon as it is understood that they are identical, it is seen that together they constitute an infinite set. They constitute a self-determined unity, a negation of negation: when we negate the something, we get the something else, and when the something else is negated, we get back to the original, that is, to the something.

The true infinite is thus a combination of the finite and the infinite. Or rather, the finite is absorbed into the infinite and therefore ceases to exist as a finite element.[28] In other words, whatever is must be understood in terms of the true infinity. Whatever is experienced as being finite thus turns out by necessity to be part of the true infinite. This conceptual fact, the fact that the finite is the infinite, proves, according to Hegel, the truth of idealism.[29]

The fact that the finite must be conceived in terms of the infinite implies that idealism can be explained in the following way: The finite, con-

---

28. "Thus the finite has vanished in the infinite and what *is*, is only the *infinite*" (*SL* 138).

29. "The proposition that the finite is ideal constitutes idealism. The idealism of philosophy consists in nothing else than in recognizing that the finite has no veritable being. Every philosophy is essentially an idealism or at least has idealism for its principle . . ." (*SL* 154–55). And a little later Hegel writes: "A philosophy which ascribed veritable, absolute being to finite existence as such, would not deserve the name of philosophy" (*SL* 155). In Hegel's view, any kind of dependence on anything else makes something "ideal"; mind-dependence is thus a subspecies of such dependence. Cf. also K.R. Westphal, *Hegel's Epistemological Realism* (Dordrecht: Kluwer, 1989), ch. 10.

ceived as some particular (i.e., as nonuniversal), can neither be described nor be an object of knowledge. Or rather, it can be described as known only in terms of universals. Any attribute or property used in a description must necessarily be a universal. An attribute or a property that is not conceived as a universal would be meaningless. The existence of the particular as such is only a myth.

Because the something is identified in and through the something else, that is, identified with that which negates the negation of the something and consequently falls under the category of being-for-self, it is an expression of being a unity—of being. Hegel calls it "the one." Another way of expressing it would be to say that the something and the something else have the same denotation: The something and the something else constitute the same entity. But with respect to connotation, the something and the something else are different; their connotations form two different concepts. In this connection, Hegel uses (quite misleadingly) the expressions 'repulsion' and 'attraction'. In connection with identity, that is, with the one and therefore with the concept of denotation, Hegel uses the term 'attraction', whereas he uses the concept of 'repulsion' in connection with the difference between the connotation of the two concepts.[30]

Hegel maintains that the one (that is, the denotation) enjoys logical priority over the connotation (which, analogously, he calls the many). He does not much explain why this is so. He may draw on a philosopher like Plotinus, who thought that the many were emanation from the one. But Plotinus' theory was an ontological or cosmological theory, whereas Hegel's logic is a conceptual investigation—an investigation according to which the connotation of a concept results from philosophical analysis. The something else is a negation of the something and consequently presupposes the something, that is, the one. And because the one has logical priority, it follows that repulsion has logical priority over attraction; attraction presupposes repulsion.[31]

---

30. "We will in fact see that Hegel not infrequently uses language of physical alteration to express conceptual entailments," Crawford Elder, *Appropriating Hegel* (Aberdeen: Aberdeen University Press, 1980), 5. That Hegel does not conceive of repulsion and attraction as physical forces is obvious. He calls repulsion a figurative term, and he adds: "we must not interpret this process of repulsion to mean that the One is *what repels* while the many are *what is repelled*; instead, as we said earlier, it is the One that is just what excludes itself from itself and posits itself as what is many . . ." (*Enz.* §97 Addition).

31. "The relation of attraction to repulsion is such that the former has the latter

Because the something else is a negation of the something (the one), then whatever falls under the negation belongs to the many. If the something is, say, green, then the something else (the many) is that which is not green but either blue or red or yellow, and so on, each of which itself is a one. As Hegel puts it, "each of the many, however, is itself a one," and he then adds "and because it behaves as such, this all-round repulsion turns over forthwith into its opposite—*attraction*" (*Enz.* §97 Addition).

The use of the terms 'repulsion' and 'attraction', when applied within the sphere of conceptual analysis—within the category of being-for-self—in many respects says no more and no less (although misleadingly) than the term 'negation' when used in connection with the difference between denotation and connotation. The one expresses the being-for-self when the identity of denotation is emphasized, and the many express the being-for-other when differences of connotation are emphasized. We thereby avoid the danger of being misled when we speak about the repulsion and attraction as if they were processes, as something taking place—which would be absurd. Nor would we need any arguments in order to show that repulsion and attraction are in fact identical. We would not need any such arguments because we do not employ these concepts.[32] The relation between concepts is a logical one. In that relation, the concepts of repulsion and attraction apply only in a figurative sense, and even then only in a misleading way.

Hegel never forgot his Greek forebears, and the influence of ancient philosophy is traceable in almost everything he wrote. The concepts of the one and the many are themes in Anaximander's cosmology and, more elaborately, in the cosmology of Plotinus. Nevertheless, while Plotinus' emanation is a cosmological concept, Hegel's concepts of repulsion and attraction cancel each other and leave us with a conceptual investigation. From Anaximander and Plotinus to Hegel, we witness how, in the hands of philosophy, cosmology changes into conceptual logic.

for a *presupposition*. Repulsion provides the material for attraction" (*SL* 173).

32. As mentioned in note 30, Hegel is using the physical language—what Carnap called the "material mode of speech"—when for instance he talks about attraction and repulsion. Instead of talking about the timeless conceptual relation, he speaks about the *process* of the repelling of the many, and the *process* of the attraction of the many to the one. His conclusion makes it clear, however, that what he is speaking of does not involve physical entities, but conceptions and their relations—as when for instance he says that "being-for-self (in the two sides of its process, repulsion and attraction) has proved itself to be the sublating of itself . . ." (*Enz.* §98 Addition).

note: I've said the logic traces the becoming of - a - science of logic, which suggests a becoming - legitimate or a becoming - concepts of the 'concepts' of logic. In a way though all these 'concepts' are also on their way from being (mere) concepts to being true, or true concepts, &c. concepts but are true of being.

Quantity

Pure Quantity and Quantum   *? woory headed*
Continuity and Discreteness

When we move to the category of quantity, we find again the characteristically Hegelian structure of analysis. That is, we find the all-important concept of negation; this concept is implied by the cognitive fact that a thing is identical with—its identity conditions are interdefined with—that which it is not. We therefore also find the concept of true infinity.

In quality, we found that the something and the something else constitute the root of the false or bad infinity, which in turn, when corrected, became the true infinity and hence the category of being-for-self. Finally, we saw that being-for-self led to the one and the many, which Hegel explicates with the concepts of repulsion and attraction. These two concepts, as I showed, annulled each other, but in the category of quantity, we find that the dialectical tension between the concepts of the one and the many expresses itself in the concepts of continuity and discreteness (*Diskretion*).

An essential difference between quality and quantity is this: If we change the quality of a certain thing, we thereby change the identity of that thing. But the quantity of a thing can be changed without thereby changing the quality of it. I can make a thing bigger or smaller without thereby changing it into another kind of thing. If I change the size of a pair of shoes, it is still a pair of shoes; but if the quality of a thing is changed (I may turn the shoes into a pair of slippers), then their being is changed; they consequently cease to be shoes.

from quality comes infinity

So, quantity falls outside "being"? But this is the logic of Being! Aren't you saying 'being' when you mean existence (a category of Essence)?

27

Hegel distinguishes between pure quantity and quantum. By pure quantity, he understands an indeterminate quantity, whereas by a quantum, he understands a determinate quantity. To speak about space as such or about time as such is to speak about pure quantity. However, if I speak about the volume of a certain box, this is a quantum. There is an answer to the question how big the box is; but to talk about space as such or about time as such is not to talk about a certain part of space or a certain period of time. Or if I say that there were many people in the street, I speak in terms of quantity, indeed a pure quantity. I have not committed myself to answer the question about how many people there in fact were.

The two concepts, the one and the many, Hegel tied to the concepts of repulsion and attraction, but, as we saw, these two concepts annulled each other. However, when we move into the category of quantity, we are introduced to the concepts of continuity and discreteness. These two concepts are both abstract, that is metaphysical, and necessary. To say that they are abstract and metaphysical is to say that they are conceptually derived and therefore not empirically ascertained; to say that they are necessary follows from the fact that they are logically built into the concept of quantity. Hegel is anxious to emphasize, however, that although both concepts (continuity and discreteness) by necessity apply to any quantity, they do not apply simultaneously; it is an either/or—one or the other concept must be applied.

A typical example of pure quantity, as mentioned earlier, is space. It is in the nature of a pure quantity, such as space (for instance as demonstrated by a straight line) to continue, to transcend itself, and thereby to produce itself. A straight line does not, by its very nature, come to a stop; its nature is to be without end. It is self-producing. As Hegel expresses it: "Space, time and the rest, are expansion, pluralities which are a coming-out-of-self, a flowing which, however, does not pass over into its opposite, into quality or the one" (*SL* 189). Its continuation is built into it. It is as if there is nothing that stops it; it is part of its very nature to outgrow itself, to prolong itself beyond any point it reaches. The concept of continuity and the concept of discreteness are perhaps the two most important concepts under the category of quantity. They are equally necessary. Any quantity has both continuity and discreteness. Discreteness presupposes that there is something of which the discrete is a discrete unit—just as a piece of cake presupposes the cake of which it is a piece. And, *vice versa*, the cake presupposes the concept of discreteness. It does not mean that there already are pieces cut out from the cake; there may or may not be. The point is that, although the cake may not be divided, it is obviously divisible; in fact, it is infinitely divisible. This infinity is, of course, a bad infinity; it is logically impossible that it should ever be completed. There is no logical route leading from the statement "X is infinitely divisible" to the statement "X is infinitely divided." One reason for this is that the latter statement in fact is no genuine statement. To be infinitely divided would imply that there were an infinite number of parts, which clearly would be not false but nonsensical. However much a quantity is divided, we shall never be able to transcend a finite number of parts or elements.

In general, we may say that the concept of part (the discrete) presupposes the concept of a whole (the continuous, that is, the whole of which the part is a part). There must always be an answer to the question: What is the part a part of? And, *vice versa*, the concept of continuity presupposes the concept of a part, that is, the parts resulting from the infinite divisibility. In other words, the concepts of a part (the discrete, the many) and of the whole (the continuous, the one) presuppose each other. Or, if one prefers, the logical syntax of the language-game of discreteness, L_d, is different from the logical syntax of the language-game of continuity, L_c. But L_d and L_c presuppose each other. L_d can be used only if L_c forms the logical background, just as L_c can be used only if L_d forms the logical background. If we use one of these language-games without the other as a logical background, we land ourselves in paradoxes.

This syntactical rule, the rule that the use of L_d requires the logical background of L_c, is violated by Zeno when he by apparent necessity deduced his famous paradoxes about the logical impossibility of motion. The arrow will never reach the goal aimed at because it is impossible for the arrow to move. The line that represents the trajectory over the distance from the starting point to the goal is a continuous line. And as a continuous line it is also discrete, which implies that it can be divided into meters, centimeters, millimeters, or whatever. Each of these can again be divided, and so on *ad infinitum*—a bad infinity. We shall never reach a last unit, that is, a unit where we cannot continue the division, or rather where the claim that we could not continue the division would have no meaning. The distance between the starting point and the goal, that is, the length of the trajectory, does not consist of so and so many meters or centimeters in the same way in which a wall consists of so many bricks. The path does not *consist* of meters or centimeters; it *measures* so and so many meters. According to L_c the trajectory is so-and-so long. The trajectory, the line, is measured to be so-and-so long; the parts—the meters or centimeters or whatever unit is used—presuppose the whole (parts must always be parts of something, in this case the parts are parts of the trajectory line). The discrete presupposes the continuous. But if we cut loose the discrete from the continuous and consequently ignore that L_d presupposes L_c, then the parts are not conditioned by the continuous and, consequently, do not satisfy the logical condition for being parts. They can be parts only if they are parts of a whole. To be discrete is, necessarily, to be discrete units of the continuous. To be many is to be many of one. Zeno, therefore, can continue his division of the trajectory without being logically hindered by the continuous (the one or the whole). He is logically free, therefore, to assume that the trajectory does not *measure* so-and-so many meters or centimeters, but *consists* of points. And because the line does not consist of a finite number of points—it would be nonsense to say that a ten-meter line consists of, say, two thousand or two billion points—then to assume that a line consists of points, must mean that it consists of infinitely many points. And if the arrow has to pass an infinite number of points, then the arrow will never move. But as we have seen, the transition (or inference) from being infinitely divisible to being infinitely divided is an incorrect transition (inference), which results in a nonsensical assumption. It is likewise based on an incorrect use of 'consist of' or 'is composed of'. This use leads to the assumption that points are parts of a line.

That this is not the case can be seen from the following example. Take a line AB. One half of the line is blue, the other half is yellow. Let M be the middle point. Therefore, every point on the line to the left of M is blue and every point to the right is yellow. Now where does the blue color begin, and where does the yellow color begin? The obvious answer seems to be at M. But what color is M itself? If we say that M is blue it follows that M is to the left of the middle point, that is, the middle point is not the middle point; and to say that it is yellow is to say that M is to the right of the middle point and therefore cannot be the middle point. The middle point thus seems to disappear.[33]

If Zeno had not divorced L_d from L_c, and used only L_d, thus divorced from the use of the concept of 'part', he would not have been led to use the concept of 'consist of' or 'composed of'; he would instead have been logically forced to use the concept of measure. Moreover, the concept of

33. Cf. my article "Movement, Moments, and Beginning" (*op. cit.*), pp. 74f, 78.

measure does not permit the use of the concept of 'point'. It has no meaning
to measure a point or to say that a line measures so many points—nor, consequently, to say that a line measures infinitely many points.

Number

To move from quantity to quantum is to move from the indeterminate to the determinate. A quantum has a definite volume, a definite
length, a definite weight, and so on. A quantum thus is limited, and its
limit must be expressible as a number.

Whereas a pure quantity has continuity (i.e., its continuity is not interrupted by a limit), the continuity of a quantum is just that: it is interrupted
by being limited. As Hegel puts it: "as a result the quantum also breaks up at
the same time into an indeterminate multitude of quanta or determinate
magnitudes. Each of these determinate magnitudes, as distinct from the
others, forms a unit, just as, considered all by itself, it is a many. And in this
way quantum is determined as *number*" (*Enz.* §10 Addition).

To limit pure quantity is to make it into a quantum; it is, according to
the Spinozistic principle, to negate it; it is to determine it.

The concept of limit is thus logically connected with the concept of
negation and the concept of number. The limit provides the answer to
questions like: How much? How long? How heavy? The answers to such
questions are numbers. It is necessary, however, to distinguish between two
moments of numbers: a number expressing an amount (*Anzahl*) and a
number expressing a unit (*Zahl*). When a child is asked to count to ten,
each number he mentions is a unit. But if he answers a question about how
many apples he has, then the number he mentions as an answer to the question is a number, that is, the number of the amount of apples he has. If he
finds out how many apples he has by counting and the last number he arrives at is ten, then this number is used both as a unit and as an amount. Or
in general, if one counts objects in order to find an answer to the question
How many?, then each number mentioned in the counting process is used
as a unit, and the last number (the limiting number) expresses the amount.

To say that there are ten apples in the basket, that is, to say that the
amount of the apples is ten, is to say that the amount represents a discrete
magnitude. It is a countable magnitude of ten apples. The numbers, as
units, have epistemological priority over numbers as amounts. The units
are the ones I use in counting, and without this process I could not have
knowledge of any amount. (It is irrelevant that for small amounts I do not
need to count.)

Extensive and Intensive Magnitudes

Within a quantum, Hegel distinguishes between what he calls an extensive and an intensive magnitude.

To say about a quantum that it is an extensive magnitude is to say that it is measurable. If I say about a quantum that its length is ten yards, this means that yard follows upon yard until one reaches the end, the tenth yard (ten being the limiting number). I can make sure—I can verify—that the length is ten yards by counting all the yards. I count all the units. By performing the act of counting, I treat the quantum as an extensive quantum. All the units in an extensive quantum are, so to speak, inside the quantum. Of course, they are not there in a physical sense; their presence means that whenever I want to, I can count and recount the units.

I can also treat the number 10 as an expression of an amount.

There is a difference between a number expressing an amount and what Hegel calls a degree. In the number of an amount—the number expressing an amount of yards, feet, inches, volume, and the like—the unit numbers are potentially extensive. They are absorbed into the number of the amount, but they can be recounted as extensive. However, if we talk about a degree, for instance a room temperature of 20°C, then the degrees below the 20°C never formed an extensive magnitude that was absorbed in that degree of temperature, in this case 20°C. The degree cannot be verified by adding the degrees below 20°—as we can add the yards in order to verify the correctness of a length. In a room temperature of 20°C, the degrees below 20°C simply are not there to be added up.

A degree has intensity; a number has a numerical value but cannot meaningfully be said to have intensity. The criterion for the correctness of the number of an amount is the measurement. The criterion for the correctness of the degree is not the thermometer. Of course, I can measure the degree with the thermometer; I can count the degrees on the scale of the thermometer; nevertheless, such a measurement, such a counting on the scale, cannot constitute the criterion. Suppose I find the temperature of the room pleasant. I check the thermometer and find that it reads not 20°C, but only 2°C. I most certainly shall not think that I am mistaken in finding the temperature pleasant. Note the absurdity of the following statement: "I thought I found it pleasant, but that must be a mistake; I should really be most unpleasantly freezing." What I will do, of course, is to have my thermometer repaired.

Any quantum is both an extensive and an intensive magnitude. If I take a stone in my hand, I sense both temperature and weight. Both of these sensations have a degree. They are expressions of the stone as an intensive magnitude; but I can also measure, by help of instruments, the stone's temperature and its weight. The mercury column in the thermometer has risen to the number 20. The mercury column is thus an extensive magnitude. Likewise, if I place the stone on a scale, I see that the indicator on the scale moves up to a certain number, which then constitutes the weight of the stone.

But precisely because any quantum is both an extensive and an intensive magnitude, some philosophers have maintained—in the spirit of a Galileo—that all intensive magnitudes, being subjective, should be conceived as and translated into extensive magnitudes. Because they are 'objective' and measurable and therefore verifiable, these latter are more scientific. Such a physicalistic theory, however, Hegel opposes. This is, he claims, to go beyond the sphere of perception and experience and to rely on a metaphysical theory (materialism)—a theory Hegel rejects (*Enz.* §103 Addition). It would furthermore be a rejection of what we mean when we speak of intensive magnitudes. If we speak about a color, what we speak about is the experience (the perception) of the color and not about certain noncolored physiological processes (processes we do not see).

Quantitative Infinity

Measure

A quantum is a quantum precisely because it has a particular size. It is limited. Its size is measurable by help of the number series. The numbers are used partly to count the size, the length, the volume, and the like, of the quantum; that is, it is used to count the units. It is used as a number. And partly it is used, not to count the units, but to express the results of the counting; it is used to give the amount. It is the limiting number.

It is part of the logic of the numerical series that it is infinite (a bad infinity). It is unstoppable and endless. Take any number, say, the number 5. This number is not understood unless it is understood as being the successor of the number 4 and the predecessor of the number 6. In general, the understanding of any number is conditioned by the understanding of its predecessor, just as its successor is understood only if it is understood that it is the successor of its predecessor. Because each number for its meaning and its existence depends on the meaning and existence of the neighboring numbers, it follows that the numerical series is logically endless.

A quantum has, however, a limited size. It is limited by the neighboring quantum. The limit delimiting one quantum from its neighbor is the limiting number. That is, the limiting number marks the end of one quantum and the beginning of the next quantum. But because the numerical series is endless, it follows that the series of quanta is endless, that is, a series that is a bad infinity.

To say that there are two neighboring quanta is to say that they are separated by a limit. Insofar as we are dealing with quanta conceived in terms of numbers, we can have no reason for drawing the limit in one place rather than another. That would be an arbitrary choice. Because the way we in fact divide our quanta is not arbitrary, it follows that there must be a criterion other than the concept of quantum, namely the concept of quality.

Recall that the category of quality was seen to be identical with the two concepts of repulsion and of attraction and seen to be identical with the concepts of the many and of the one. It was also seen that because the concepts of repulsion and of attraction turned out to be identical, so also were the concepts of the many and of the one. This identity marks the transition from the category of quality to the category of quantity. A length, a meter stick for instance, is a one. But it is divided into 100 cm; it is therefore also a many.

Because a quantum is logically inseparable from the number system, it is logically forced to continue itself indefinitely. The term 'logically' must be emphasized in this context. It emphasizes that the numerical series has meaning only if it is understood that it is endless and that in order to have meaning each number depends, in the last analysis, on all the numbers in the number series. What is true of the number series is also true of the quanta. A quantum continues into another quantum. It pushes itself beyond itself. In the *Logic,* Hegel expresses it thus: "The quantum which, in its otherness, is identical with itself and which determines the beyond of itself, has reached the stage of being-for-self" (*SL* 321).

As we know from the categories of quality, the difference between bad infinity and true infinity is that true infinity falls under the category of being-for-self. This is precisely what we have in the system of the progressing quanta.

In the *Encyclopaedia,* Hegel puts it this way: "In its determinacy of *being on its own account* quantum *is external* to itself. This self-externality constitutes its *quality*; it is in this very self-externality that it is itself and is related to itself. In this way, the externality, i.e., the quantitative, and the being-for-self, the qualitative, are united" (*Enz.* §105). And in comment on the same section, Hegel elaborates: "The quantitative infinite progress appears at first as a perpetual projection of numbers beyond themselves.

However, when we look more closely, it turns out that in this progression quantity returns to itself, for the thought that is contained in it is in any event the determination of number by number . . ." (*Enz.* §105 Addition).

Under the category of measure, however, we finally see how the category of quality, in its sublated form, is integrated into the category of quantity.

The category of measure is the last category under the category of quantity. And as we have just seen, the category of quality, despite its apparent discrepancy with the category of quantity (to change the quality of a certain determinate being is to change the very determinate being, that is, to change it into another kind of determinate being, although to change the quantity of a determinate being is not, at least not necessarily, to change the determinate being into another kind of determinate being), nevertheless turns out to be applicable and, indeed, necessarily applicable.

The category of measure is the category that determines the logical relation between the categories of quantity and quality. It therefore also shows why the alleged bad infinity is a true infinity.[34] As Hegel says: "Abstractly expressed, in measure quality and quantity are united" (*SL* 327).

In one place Hegel writes: "We can also consider measure as a definition of the Absolute, and it has been said accordingly that God is the measure of all things. That is also why this intuition forms the keynote of many ancient Hebrew psalms, where the glorification of God essentially comes down to saying that it is *he* who has appointed for everything its limit, for the sea and the dry land, the rivers and the mountains, and equally for the various kinds of plants and animals" (*Enz.* §107 Addition). What this means is not just that the size of human beings, plants, and the like, is within limits, and if the limits are transcended, the quality of the thing changes (the plant may then be a tree, the river—if too small—a stream, etc.). What is of primary importance and relevance in this context is the measure determining the logical relation between the quantity and quality.

---

34. It is generally agreed that Hegel's treatment of 'measure' in the *Logic* is far from clear. The various commentators' comments on Hegel's treatment of this particular category range from "very complex" (Taylor) to "one of the most difficult and obscure of Hegel's writings" (Findlay), not to mention Errol E. Harris's comment in his book *An Interpretation of the Logic of Hegel*: "On this topic the greater Logic is so obscure as to be, for the most part, hardly intelligible." The treatment of the category of measure is not only more condensed, but reaches a higher degree of intelligibility. My exposition here relies mostly, but not exclusively, on the *Encyclopaedia*.

The category of measure concerns the mutual dependency between the category of quality and the category of quantity.

An example often used to illustrate the relation (the measure) between quality and quantity is the changing temperature of some water. If the temperature is between 0°C and 100°C, there is no qualitative change, but if the temperature rises above 100°C or falls below 0°C, the quality changes to, respectively, steam or ice. There can be quantitative changes in the temperature of the water that do not occasion qualitative changes. Only when the temperature exceeds the bounds of the measure—namely, either 100°C or 0°C—do the qualitative changes occur. Even though quantitative changes occur continuously, they occur by degrees; qualitative changes occur suddenly.[35]

Hegel's use of such examples has been criticized for relying on empirical facts, that is, on what is contingently true instead of being true by conceptual necessity. W.T. Stace, for instance, writes: "The deduction draws its plausibility only from the empirical examples, such as the change of water into steam. Without this illegitimate appeal to experience the deduction would break down."[36] Such a criticism apparently forgets that, although it is an empirical fact that, for example, the limits of the measure of water is 0°C and 100°C, the category of measure is not based on experience. It is based on the logical fact that any determinate being is both a qualitative and a quantitative magnitude and that the category of measure unites the concepts of quality and quantity. Every determinate being is therefore both a continuous and a discrete magnitude. Thus, it is a conceptual necessity that qualitative changes occur according to the principle of discreteness, whereas quantitative changes occur according to the princi-

---

35. "Water when its temperature is altered does not merely get more or less hot but passes through from the liquid into either the solid or gaseous states; these states do not appear gradually; on the contrary, each new state appears as a leap, suddenly interrupting and checking the gradual succession of temperature changes at these points" (*SL* 369). In the *Encyclopaedia*, Hegel puts it this way: "Thus, for instance, the temperature of water is, up to a point, indifferent in relation to its liquid state; but there comes a point in the increasing or decreasing of the temperature of liquid water where this state of cohesion changes qualitatively, and the water is transformed into steam, on the one hand, and ice, on the other. When a quantitative alteration takes place it appears, to start with, to be something quite innocent; but something quite different lurks behind it, and this seemingly innocent alteration of the quantitative is like a ruse with which to catch the qualitative" (*Enz.* §108 Addition).

36. W. T. Stace, *The Philosophy of Hegel* (London: Macmillan, 1924), 172f.

ple of continuity. The qualitative leap is consequently not based on experience but is deduced from the logical system. That this is the case is clearly stated by Findlay in his Foreword to Wallace's translation of the *Encyclopaedia*: "These doctrines are not interesting if treated as mere 'facts of life' as they have been by some Marxists: Hegel makes them interesting by arguing that they are necessarily true."[37]

If a quantity transgresses the limit of the measure of the quality, that quantity disappears and the quantity is, so to speak, set free from that quality but is instantly connected with a new quality. Quantity is a continuous magnitude; thus, by necessity, it must be a transgressing magnitude—an endless series in the same way the number series is endless. But as just emphasized, any determinate being is both a quantitative and a qualitative magnitude; the category of measure therefore always and necessarily applies, that is to say, measure *is* a category.

Hegel says that the series passes from measure over measureless (*masslos*) to new measure. This series is of course a bad infinity. True infinity, however, is this: The quantitative changes occur according to the principle of continuity, whereas the qualitative changes occur according to the principle of discreteness. Because of the qualitative changes—leaps—the determinate being passes from measure over measureless to new measure. However, it is a conceptual necessity, known since ancient Greek philosophy, that there can be no change unless there is something that does not change. That which does not change—atoms in Democritus' philosophy or substance in Aristotle's metaphysics and in Descartes' philosophy—Hegel calls "the perennial substrate."[38]

The relation between the quantitative alterations and the qualitative leaps Hegel compares to a nodal line. The continuous line between the nodes is the continuity of the quantitative processes, and the nodes represent the qualitative leaps. The allegedly measureless points are thus the nodal points on the line. It is obvious, however, that this analogy may

---

37. *Op. cit.*, xx.

38. "In measure, the thing itself is already in itself the unity of its qualitative and quantitative moments, the two moments which constitute the element of difference within the general sphere of being and of which one is the beyond of the other; in this way the perennial substrate has directly in its own self the determination of affirmative infinity. This self-sameness of the substrate is *posited* in the fact that the qualitative self-subsistence measures into which the specifying unity is dispersed consist only of quantitative differences, so that the substrate continues itself into this differentiation of itself" (*SL* 372).

mislead. It may mislead if it is taken to imply that the node is not just a mathematical point on the line, but is a point in the sense that it is a point (however small) of the line. If this were the case, then there would be a moment (however short) when there is a quantum without a quality: the old quality has perished and the new quality is not yet there. But this is a conceptual impossibility. It is an impossibility in the same way as it is an impossibility that, say, the big hand on the clock, insofar as its movement is a continuous movement, should ever *be* at any point, if by "point" we understand a mathematical point. For any such point, it must be true that the big hand either has not yet been there or has passed it; at no time can it correctly be said that it *is* there. Of course, the truth is that a mathematical point is not an ontological concept in the sense that a line or a circle can be said to consist of such points.[39]

As we know from the category of quality, the difference between bad infinity and true infinity is that only true infinity falls under the category of being-for-self.

What guarantees the unity of the quantitative processes and the qualitative leaps is the substrate.[40] Quantitative changes, qualitative leaps, and the category of measure are the important concepts that constitute any instance of being-for-self. Therefore, being-for-self constitutes the true infinity of measure: Every change that occurs within the unity is guaranteed to be continuous by the substrate and the category of measure. Every change—quantitative alteration or qualitative leap—is related to one and the same substrate. It is a closed system that expresses being-for-self.

The category of quality, as we have seen, implies the category of

---

39. Hegel explicitly holds, however, that there is no time-gap between one quality and the next one. He thus says: "But now, when the quantity that is present in measure exceeds a certain limit, the corresponding quality is thereby sublated, too. What is negated in this way, however, is not quality in general, but only this determinate quality, whose place is immediately taken again by another one" (*Enz.* §109 Addition). In the *Logic*, Hegel expresses it thus: "the new measure relation into which the original one passes is, with respect to this, measureless, but in its own self it is equally a quality on its own account" (*SL* 371).

40. "The quantitative reference beyond itself to an other which is itself quantitative perishes in the emergence of a measure relation, of a quality; and the qualitative transition is sublated in the very fact that the new quality is itself only a quantitative relation. This transition of the qualitative and the quantitative into each other proceeds on the basis of their unity, and the meaning of the process is only to *show* or to *posit* the *determinate being* of such a substrate underlying the process, a substrate which is their unity" (*SL* 372–73).

being-for-self, which in turn implies the concepts of one and many and the concepts of repulsion and attraction. But because these concepts coalesced, quality had to be sublated into quantity. Instead of the one and the many and the implied repulsion and attraction, we got the concepts of discreteness and continuity and of extensive and intensive magnitudes. As we also have seen, an essential difference between quality and quantity is that even though a change of quality of a determinate being changes it into another kind of determinate being, a change of quantity does not: It remains the same kind of determinate being.

This essential difference between quality and quantity is consistent with the fact that a magnitude can be determined both qualitatively and quantitatively. Furthermore, as the analysis of the category of measure has shown, any magnitude must by necessity allow both quantitative changes and qualitative leaps. Precisely because this conceptual duality has necessity, it leads to the next category. It leads us from being to essence.

Summary

Everyone grants this first part of Hegel's *Logic* is not easy to comprehend; a summary of some of the main points in the deduction may therefore be useful.

One of the most important concepts in Hegel's philosophy is the concept of negation. That concept is, so to speak, the foundation of Hegel's logic. Negativity is a necessary condition for determination. This concept leads us from pure being, and thus from nothing and becoming, to determinate being. Being is determined by having some quality. The general expression for determinate being, that is, to have some quality, is to be something. But a 'something' is only determinate by being distinct from 'something else'. To say now that this something else itself has to be determined by some third thing, would generate what Hegel calls bad infinity. True infinity is this: The 'something else' which determines 'something' is its negation. As a trivial example, consider the color blue. If one says about something that it is blue, that is only understood if one thereby knows what it is not. It is not red, not yellow, not green, in fact no other color than blue. Hence, one may say, the color blue is identical with the color that all other colors are not or, if one prefers, every something is "identical" with something else—in the sense that the identity conditions of anything are interdefined with the identity conditions of other, distinct things—and this something else is the negation of 'something', that is, the negation of the 'something' to which the 'something else' in question corresponds.

'Something', in other words, and the corresponding 'something else' are 'identical', in the sense that their identity conditions are interdefined. That means that what determines 'something' is itself; it is self-determining. True infinity consists in identity between 'something' and 'something else'. One may therefore say that 'something' both differs from and is identical with 'something else'. In explicating this seemingly contradictory statement, I have used Frege's distinction between denotation and connotation. The expressions "morning star" and "evening star" are identical in the sense that they denote the very same planet, but differ in having different connotations (the word 'morning' means, as everyone knows, something else than the word 'evening'). In connection with Hegel's philosophy, it must be stressed that the connotations of the relevant sets of concepts do not merely differ. They are mutually opposed and interdefined, and the use of either concept logically requires the use of the other.

A necessary (though not a sufficient) condition of understanding Hegel is to understand what it means to say that something is "identical" with what this something is not, and that one understands what Hegel means by the concept of true infinity. If one does not understand this, one will not understand Hegel.

Being, besides quality, is determined by quantity. Quality and quantity appear independent of each other. By changing the size of something, one does not change its quality. If one takes in or lets out a gown, it still is a gown; but if one changes the quality, the gown becomes something else, for example, a bunch of rags.

A consequence of true infinity is the category of being-for-self. In applying this category, one understands that negation is identical with what is negated. One of the ways in which Hegel puts this is to say that it is negation of negation: That which negates absorbs that which is negated, and makes it, so to speak, identical with itself. In being-for-self that which negates is negated in such a way that it becomes identical with what it negates. Hence, the category of being-for-self, which presupposes negation and true infinity, is also a necessary condition for understanding Hegel.

Hegel's analysis of the category of quantity shows that quality and quantity are not as independent of each other as one would initially suppose. The analysis of the last category, the category of measure, shows not merely that they are not independent of each other; it shows that they form a unity while they all the same also are both identical and different.

Essence

Essence as Mediated Being

The truth of being is essence. Essence, therefore, is the knowledge of the necessity of the way being presents itself. Being presents itself immediately, whereas essence is mediated—sublated—being. To know the essence is to know what is essential and that is to know the truth of being. But to have the concept of the essential entails the concept of the unessential; or, which is the same, the mediated entails the immediate, and vice versa. Immediate being—the way being presents itself—Hegel calls 'show' (*Schein*).[41] The philosophical task is to move from show to essence. This task is completed when show has been incorporated into essence, that is, show has moved from the unessential to the essential, from the immediate to the mediated. But since being thus has become mediated being, and the unessential consequently has become essential, it follows that the distinction between the essential and the unessential is eliminated. Nevertheless, the concepts of show and essence are necessary concepts. Any scientific investigation presupposes that there is a difference between show or appearance and that which shows or appears. If we did not have these concepts there would be no science, and our language could not even formulate a cognitive task.

The conceptual move from show to essence or from the immediate to

---

41. Miller translates the German word *Schein* as "illusory being." It seems to me, however, that this translation is misleading. It implies that immediate being is false; but it turns out that, after the truth of being has been arrived at, the unessential is incorporated into the essential and therefore cannot be false. I therefore prefer the translation of *Schein* as 'show', which is also how W. H. Johnston and L. G. Struthers translate it.

the mediated, Hegel—influenced by the science of optics—calls reflection. Just as a light ray is reflected back from a mirror, so the mediated being returns to the immediate being, or immediate being is reflected from the mediated back to the immediate.[42] Hegel emphasizes that the conceptual movement from the mediated is a movement of being itself. There is nothing outside being that occasions the mediation.[43] This reflection Hegel calls 'to recollect' (*zu erinnern*). But he also calls it 'to inwardize' (*zu er-innern*). Such remarks are, of course, too general to be informative, or rather, they are misleading because they suggest that the process is psychological. Obviously, essence as such is not becoming in the sense of a temporal process.[44] What is temporal, however, is the scientific investigation aiming at the discovery of the essence of this or that, of the truth about this or that or, if one prefers, the discovery of the laws of various phenomena. Such an investigation presupposes that the essence is there to be discovered. But to emphasize again: Hegel's purpose is to map out conceptual relations. It is not an empirical investigation; it may, however, be said to be to lay out the conceptual framework for empirical investigations.

The becoming of essence Hegel describes rather provocatively as a "movement of nothing to nothing, and so back to itself" (*SL* 400). In order to get a clearer picture of the meaning of this statement, consider again the concept of negation as it functions in the category of quality. According to the Spinozistic principle, it is impossible to move from pure being to determinate being except by using the concept of negation. That is, the concept of negation is a necessary condition for having the concept of 'something'.

---

42. "The standpoint of essence is in general the standpoint of reflection. The term 'reflection' is primarily used of light, when, propagated rectilinearly, it strikes a mirrored surface and is thrown back by it. So we have here something twofold: first, something immediate, something that is, and second, the same as mediated or posited" (*Enz.* §112 Addition).

43. "But this path is the movement of being itself. It was seen that being inwardizes itself through its own nature, and through this movement into itself becomes essence" (*SL* 389).

44. Hegel heeds the fact that the German language has preserved the term "*Wesen*" (the German term for 'essence') in the past participle, "*gewesen.*" Analogously, light rays move from the mediated and return to the immediate after having been conceptualized, and thus conceptualized, the immediate being becomes mediated, that is, becomes essence. That this movement to and fro is a timeless process Hegel indicates thus: "The German language has preserved essence in the past participle [*gewesen*] of the verb *to be*; for essence is past—but time timelessly past—being" (*SL* 389).

Recall, too, that 'something' is understood only through its negation. That is, 'something' is understood only through 'something else'. According to the categories of true infinity and being-for-self, 'something else' is identical with 'something'. The 'something' is that which it is not. Another way to express the same relation is to say that 'something' negates itself—it is its own negation. Likewise, 'something else' is its own negation; it negates itself. This relation—the relation of quality—is, so to speak, a horizontal movement. In essence, the movement from immediate to mediated is a vertical movement. The immediate, the show, is the surface, and the mediated is the underlying substratum. The show is the negation of itself, and, consequently, the movement from show is a movement from nothing. Likewise, the mediated is a negation of itself, and, consequently, the movement back to show is a movement from nothing to nothing.

Identity

Show and essence, the unessential and the essential, immediate being and mediated being, have all been shown (by philosophical analysis) to be identical. Nevertheless, as emphasized earlier, these distinctions are necessary conditions for language. It is important to see, therefore, that what has been shown through philosophical analysis is not that the concepts of show and of essence are or should be eliminated. What Hegel reveals is their proper logical function. It is now seen, as mentioned earlier, that they are identical insofar as denotation is concerned but different (and opposed) insofar as connotation is concerned.

As mentioned, the concept of show is a necessary concept; it is a necessary condition for arriving at the truth of being. The path leading to the truth must by necessity start from the immediate, that is, it must begin at what in the *Phenomenology* is termed sense-certainty; it must begin at the immediately given, that is, the show, the unessential, the immediate. From sense-certainty the *Phenomenology* arrives through philosophical analysis at "the truth" of sense-certainty, that is, at the view that what constitutes the content of the so-called given is not sheer particulars (the 'here', the 'now', the 'this', the 'I') but particulars specified by universals.

But because the necessary beginning for arriving at the truth of being is immediate being, show, it follows that show or the unessential is a necessary concept for arriving at the truth of being, at the essential, at essence. In other words, the necessary path is from the immediate to the mediated and then, through reflection, back to the immediate, which is then absorbed by or incorporated into the mediated. Show thus becomes, through this process, part of essence. Show is no longer distinct from or foreign to, but rather is part of the truth. It is the face of essence.

The concept of show, as described earlier, is the necessary beginning of the process aiming at mediated being. But this concept, the concept of show, being the face of essence, must be something of which one is conscious, that is, it must already be conceptualized;[45] if it were not, it would be (logically) impossible to be conscious of it. A not yet conceptualized show does not exist; such a concept has no ontological status, it has no denotation. But just as determinate being presupposes the concept of pure being (a concept without denotation, but which has connotation), so show presupposes the concept of the not-yet-conceptualized being (i.e., the concept of pure being).

Insofar as show is identified with immediate being, the concept of immediate being cannot be identified with the concept of not-yet-conceptualized being. This concept of being is conceptualized in much the same way as the prisoners' experience was in Plato's allegory of the cave. Their experience was a show; the mediated experience, that is, the prisoners' conception of mediated being, was completed only through the knowledge achieved outside the cave. One difference between Plato's view and Hegel's is this: According to Plato, 'show' as it was conceived in the cave is necessarily false, whereas 'show' according to Hegel may or may not be false; whether it is, is a contingent matter.

Identity and Difference

Although the concept of show and the concept of essence turn out to be identical—identical in denotation—they are also different (and opposed) in connotation. In other words, the statement that show and essence are identical implies that they also are different.

This is true, according to Hegel, of all categories of reflection. Hegel distinguishes between formal identity and concrete identity. As an example of a formal identity he mentions the sentence "A planet is a planet." Such a sentence he describes as silly (*Enz.* §115 Remark). Incidentally, more than a hundred years later, Wittgenstein in his *Tractatus* characterizes such identity sentences as pseudo-propositions; and in his *Philosophical Investigations,* Wittgenstein would classify such sentences as "idling."[46]

---

45. Cf. my articles "Remarks on Experience," *Analysis* 13 (1953), 117–120; and "On Seeing," *Danish Yearbook of Philosophy* 1 (1961), 53–54.

46. L. Wittgenstein *Tractatus Logico-Philosophicus* (London: Routledge & Kegan

It is not always the case, however, that a sentence of the form 'A is A' is an empty sentence, that is, a sentence that should be classified as expressing a formal or an abstract identity. If a school teacher asks a pupil the question, "What is a planet?" and the pupil answers the question by saying "A planet is a planet," then this "answer" could in no way be regarded as an answer. If the answer instead had been, "A planet is a celestial body orbiting around the Earth," it would have been an answer, albeit mistaken.

Whether a sentence of the form 'A is A' is meaningful depends on the use of that sentence. In the preceding example, when the sentence is used to answer a question about what a planet is, it is obviously misused. But suppose somebody is wondering why Venus appears in the sky at one place in the evening and in another place in the morning; then someone else may, as an explanation, say this: "Well, Venus is a planet, and as you know, a planet is a planet and therefore orbits the Sun." Here the expression 'a planet is a planet' is used as a reminder of what a planet is. In one of Doris Days' songs she sang, "For a guy is a guy wherever he is," and here again (on a charitable interpretation) the expression 'a guy is a guy' is used as a reminder of some of the features characterizing a 'guy'.

Nevertheless, Hegel's point is clear enough. What he says about the abstract or formal identity is a criticism of the so-called laws of thought. The first of the laws of thought he expresses as 'A = A' and negatively as 'A cannot at the same time be A and not A'. Such sentences or expressions cannot possibly be regarded or used as laws of thought. 'A = A' is a tautology, and from a tautology nothing but tautologies follow.[47] In contrast to abstract identity, concrete identity is protected from being "silly" by

---

Paul, 1922), §5.35; "The confusions which occupy us arise when language is like an engine idling, not when it is doing work" (*Philosophical Investigations* I, §132).

47. Hegel does not express himself in these terms. What he does say is this: "If someone says that this proposition cannot be proven, but that *every* consciousness proceeds in accordance with it and, as experience shows agrees with it at once, as soon as it takes it in, then against this alleged experience of the Schools we have to set the universal experience that no consciousness thinks, has notions, or speaks, according to this law, and no existence of any kind at all exists in accordance with it" (*Enz.* §115). When Hegel in this quote says "that no consciousness thinks, has notions, or speaks, according to this law," he does not of course mean that the fact that no mind thinks or forms conceptions or speaks in accordance with this law is the argument against its acceptance; on the contrary, that the fact that no mind thinks this way is the result of the tautological character of the alleged law of thought; it is precisely because it is a tautology that no mind can use it to do anything but form another (and therefore empty) tautology.

containing difference. As we have already seen, in essence, the unessential and essential, the immediate and mediated, are both identical and different. Because essence is the truth of being, it is consequently also the truth of the immediate and of the unessential. In other words, concrete identity is an identity that contains, or rather is constituted by, differences.[48]

Thus essence necessarily implies identity between show and essence, between unessential and essential. Identity is therefore self-related (it is self-related because it is a relation between show and essence), but it is also a negation of itself (it is a negation of itself because the unessential is a negation of the essential). From the category of essence identity follows, and from the concept of identity difference follows. Or as has been emphasized: Identity between show and essence implies that show and essence have the same denotation; but their difference follows from the fact that the concepts of show and of essence have different connotations.

Identity necessarily presupposes that something is identical with something else (the unessential, for instance, is identical with the essential). And as we have seen, to assert that something is identical, not with something else, but with itself (to assert, for example, that a planet is a planet) transcends the limits for meaningful use of the expression "to be identical with." Incidentally, this is also the way the concept of identity is used in mathematics. If x is identical with y, that is, $x = y$, it means that x may be substituted for y when and wherever y appears. It would have no meaning to say that one may substitute x for x.

Identity implies difference and, vice versa, difference implies identity. To assert that things are different is to presuppose that there is a common standard, a standard by which to measure the difference. Thus difference presupposes identity, and identity (i.e., concrete identity) presupposes difference.

Hegel distinguishes between variety or diversity (*Verschiedenheit*) and opposition or contradiction (*Gegensatz* or *Widerspruch*). Or rather, knowledge moves from variety to opposition. 'Variety' connotes difference, where that difference is not seen as a conceptual necessity. The way to understand that the difference contains a conceptual necessity is through the concept of likeness.

---

48. As Hans-Georg Gadamer expresses it: "Everyone knows that identity would have no meaning by itself if self-sameness and differentness were not implied in it. Identity without difference would be absolutely nothing," *Hegel's Dialectic: Five Hermeneutic Studies* (New Haven: Yale University Press, 1976), 80.

A fly and a mosquito are unlike each other, but only insofar as they have something in common; they are, for instance, both insects. In other words, the concept of likeness also applies. Whenever the concept of the unlike applies, then the concept of likeness necessarily applies. The two concepts are conceptually dependent on each other.

The concepts of likeness and unlikeness have their roots in diversity or variety. But by seeing that they are based, not on external comparison but on conceptual necessity, we are no longer dealing with external likeness or unlikeness, but with identity and difference that are conceptually connected and interdependent, just as are the concepts of positivity and negativity. These two concepts are opposed, yet neither has meaning without the other; the concept of positivity presupposes the concept of negativity and vice versa. Both have applicability by conceptual necessity.[49]

Contradiction

We thus have that, since mutually opposing concepts necessarily apply, a contradiction is unavoidable.[50] And not only is it unavoidable; it is of utmost importance.[51]

Hegel has often been attacked for his acceptance and praise of contradictions and his rejection of the law of excluded middle. To maintain, as does the law of excluded middle, that everything is either A or not-A, or, in other words, that there is no third possibility, is to regard whatever is as if it enjoyed abstract or formal identity with itself (compare Hegel's remark about a statement such as "A planet is a planet"). It is not to have understood that any identity has built in its own negativity. Concrete identity involves both the essential as well as the unessential. In other words, everything is precisely "a third." Instead of being either A or not-A, it is both. It

49. "Each therefore *is*, only in so far as its *non-being* is, and is in an identical relationship with it" (*SL* 425).

50. "If, now, the first determinations of reflection, namely, identity, difference and opposition, have been put in form of a law, still more should the determination into which they pass as their truth, namely contradiction, be grasped and enunciated as a law: *everything is inherently contradictory*, and in the sense that this law in contrast to the others expresses rather the truth and the essential nature of things" (*SL* 439).

51. "[C]ontradiction is the root of all movement and vitality" (*SL* 439). By 'movement' Hegel here means conceptual movement, that is, the mapping out of the various conceptual deductions.

is both the essential and the unessential; it is both positivity and negativity.[52]

As we have just seen, in his so-called law of contradiction, Hegel says "everything is inherently contradictory" (cf. note 50 above). The contradiction built into any identity is due to the negativity that by conceptual necessity is inherent in everything. The contradiction is consequently not a defect associated with certain statements; on the contrary, it is an unavoidable (a conceptually unavoidable) feature without which we would be left with the barren and sterile abstract identity. Contradiction is the very nerve of the category of essence.

Even in a physical movement, a contradiction is present in an immediate way. In one and the same moment it is both 'here' and not 'here'. Hegel is eager to emphasize, however, that it does not follow therefore that movement does not exist. What it does show, according to Hegel, is that motion is an instance of contradiction.[53]

It is surprising that Hegel accepts this contradiction. It is surprising, considering how he was able, through an excellent conceptual analysis, to detect the conceptual fallacy behind Zeno's paradoxes. Recall that Zeno's paradoxes resulted from his failure to distinguish between the continuous and the discrete. This failure made him unable to distinguish between two different language-games, and therefore fail to distinguish the logical difference between 'consists of', 'being part of', and the logical difference

---

52. "In the positive and the negative we think we have an absolute distinction. Both terms, however, are implicitly the same. . . . There cannot be the north pole of a magnet without the south pole nor the south pole without the north pole. If we cut a magnet in two we do not have the north pole in one piece and the south pole in the other. And in the same way, positive and negative electricity are not two diverse, independently subsisting fluids" (*Enz.* §119 Addition 1). In another comment on that same paragraph Hegel writes, "Everything that is at all is concrete, and hence it is inwardly distinguished and self-opposed" (*Enz.* §119 Addition 2). Hence other commentators argue, e.g., Michael Wolff, that Hegel's view of "dialectical" contradictions neither denies nor violates the law of noncontradiction, but holds that certain important truths can only (or at least best) be expressed by using what appears to be formal contradictions. See *Der Begriff des Widerspruchs. Eine Studie zur Dialektik Kants und Hegels* (Königstein/Ts.: Hain, 1981), esp. 35–36.

53. "External, sensuous motion itself is contradiction's immediate existence. Something moves, not because at one moment it is here and at another there, but because at one and the same moment it is here and not here, because in this 'here', it at once is and is not. The ancient dialecticians must be granted the contradictions that they pointed out in motion; but it does not follow that therefore there is no motion, but on the contrary, that motion is *existent* contradiction itself" (*SL* 440).

between 'measuring units' (millimeters, centimeters, inches, etc.) and (nonextended) 'points'. It is surprising, therefore, that Hegel does not, concerning the present paradox, emphasize that the concepts of 'here' and 'moment' are either without extension in space (i.e., unextended points) and a temporally unextended moment or else are a 'here' and a 'moment' to which the concept of measure applies. In the former case, the paradox cannot arise because neither 'here' nor 'moment' is an ontological entity. A moving body (which consists of parts, but surely not of points) cannot therefore meaningfully be said to pass through a 'here' and to be 'here' at any 'moment'. Nor can the paradox arise in the latter case (i.e., the case where a 'here' and a 'moment' both have an extension).[54]

But even if we disregard the supposed contradiction associated with the concept of motion, it is still the case, as Hegel says, that whatever exists is concrete, with difference and opposition in itself, "and that contradiction is the very moving principle of the world."

---

54. See my "Movement, Moment, and Beginning" (*op. cit.*).

Ground

Ground as Unity of Identity and Difference

The category of ground is the unity of identity and difference. To repeat what has been stressed several times already: Identity, that is, both concrete and also empty and abstract identity, presuppose difference just as difference presupposes identity. Identity and difference thus presuppose each other. It is a mutual dependency; just as the positive and the negative both oppose each other, although the existence of the one depends on the existence of the other. This double-dependency Hegel regards of great importance for philosophic (*wissenschaftliche*) method as such (*SL* 323).

This mutual dependency according to which one must be used whenever the other is used implies that there is an identity between them. If A may be substituted for B and B may be substituted for A, then A and B may be regarded as identical.[55] When Hegel asserts that there is identity between difference and identity, he warns against the assumption that this new identity is an abstract identity. He consequently recommends defining the category of ground thus: "ground is not only the unity but equally the distinction of identity and distinction" (*Enz.* §121 Addition). In other words, he recommends that, instead of using the word 'identity' the word

---

55. "*Ground* is the unity of identity and distinction; the truth of what distinction and identity have shown themselves to be, the inward reflection which is just as much reflection-into-other, and vice versa. It is *essence* posited as *totality*" (*Enz.* §121).

'difference' be used, which can be done because the concrete identity implies difference just as difference implies identity.

Formal Ground, Real Ground, Sufficient Ground, Efficient Cause

The concept of ground involves by necessity two concepts: (1) that for which the ground is ground (*explicandum*) and (2) that which constitutes the ground (*explicans*). Or expressed differently, (1) is a question about a ground of something, and (2) is the answer to that question.

Hegel distinguishes between formal ground and real ground. In the formal ground, the content of the *explicandum* and the *explicans* are identical. That which *explicandum* refers to (its denotation) is the same as that which *explicans* refers to. The *explicandum* and the *explicans* have the same denotation. As an example of a formal ground, of an explanation that in fact is noninformative (it is noninformative because it explains by referring to the same phenomenon), Hegel mentions the following: If asked for the explanation of the fact that the Earth moves around the Sun, the answer is given that it is the attractive force between the Earth and the Sun; and if asked what we should understand by the attractive force, the answer is that it is the force which produces the effect that the Earth moves around the Sun. Such an answer, however, expresses only what is contained in the phenomenon of which it is supposed to be the ground (*SL* 458).

In contrast to the formal ground, where the content of the *explicandum* and the *explicans* is the same, we have no such identity in the real ground. Here *explicandum* and *explicans* refer to different phenomena. The problem then is how it is possible for one phenomenon to be explained by another phenomenon, or rather, how it is possible from one expression to imply another distinct expression, where both expressions refer to different phenomena. The derived expression is the *explicandum* (e.g., the billiard ball is rolling), while the expression that implies (and so explains) the *explicandum* is the *explicans* (e.g., the billiard ball was hit by another billiard ball). This is, of course, Hume's problem about efficient cause. Either there must be a logical identity between the two expressions, in which case we are back at the formal ground, or if not, it seems impossible, as Hume argued, to derive the one expression from the other. Our expectation that one phenomenon succeeds another phenomenon can be explained psychologically but cannot be justified epistemologically.

What is sought is what Leibniz calls the sufficient ground. But, says Hegel, the term 'sufficient' is superfluous because only a sufficient ground

52 | *An Introduction to Hegel's Logic*

qualifies as a ground. The statement, therefore, that everything has a sufficient ground is tantamount to saying that everything has a ground.[56]

When Hegel says that everything has a ground, he means that whatever does not exist immediately, but is something mediated, is something
to be explained by its ground.[57]

Obviously, Hegel would be unable to accept Hume's argument that it
would not be a logical impossibility—only difficult to believe—if a certain
event would be followed by another event contrary to what so far has been
empirically observed. According to Hegel, this would be an impossibility
because an event is only an event if it is describable and because, as he emphasizes, "the forms of thought are, in the first instance, displayed and
stored in human *language*" (*SL* 31). It is implied, among other things, that
our descriptions of different events are in terms that are expressions and
therefore are logically interconnected. This point I shall explain shortly.

One criticism Hegel makes of the concept of real ground (i.e., sufficient cause) is of special interest: When we are dealing, not with necessary
truths or tautologies where counterarguments are ruled out, but with empirical situations, a multitude of different descriptions are possible; empirical situations afford a multitude of possible applications of different
concepts. Any of the different descriptions (any of the different ways of
conceptualizing a situation) affords possibilities for different arguments or
explanations. This display of different arguments and counterarguments
is what Hegel calls 'argumentation' (*Raisonnement, Enz.* §121 Addition).[58]
This form of discussion, according to Hegel, was practiced by the Sophists, a form of discussion he defends. The purpose of the argumentation as
practiced by the Sophists was to substitute arguments, pro and con, for the
different opinions held by authority. The difference between the Sophists
and the discussions Socrates and Plato held was this: While the Sophists

56. "To add that the ground must be sufficient is really quite superfluous for it is
self-evident; that for which the ground is not sufficient would not have a ground,
but everything is supposed to have a ground" (*SL* 446).

57. "Ground, like the other determinations of reflections has been expressed in
the form of a law: Everything has its sufficient ground. This means in general nothing else but: What *is*, is not to be regarded as a merely *affirmative immediate*, but as
something *posited* . . ." (*SL* 446).

58. In *Wissenschaft der Logik* Hegel says: "Was Sokrates und Platon Sophisterei
nennen, ist nicht anderes als das Raisonnement aus Grunden" (*GW* 11; I, 311).
Both the translations by Miller and by Johnston and Struthers render it as "argumentation from grounds" (*SL* 466; Johnston and Struthers II, 94).

found arguments both pro and con, Socrates and Plato aimed at demonstrating the truth; that is, they aimed to acquire through dialectical reasoning knowledge of ideas. As Hegel says about the argumentation: "The search for and assignment of grounds, in which argumentation (*das Raisonnement*) mainly consists, is accordingly an endless pursuit which does not reach a final determination; for any and every thing one or more good grounds can be given, and also for its opposite . . ." (*SL* 466).[59]

How can the formal and the real ground be harmonized or united? How can the necessary but empirical emptiness resulting from the formal ground be harmonized or united with the content and contingency of the real ground? One alleged defect associated with real grounds is the supposed lack of epistemic connection between the event called the cause and the event called the effect. Another defect is that arguments from real grounds lead to the kind of argumentation according to which "everything can be proved by argument, and arguments for and against can be found for everything" (cf. note 59).

As we shall see when we consider Hegel's analysis of causality, he shows that cause and effect do not constitute two separate events but only one event. The problem of the missing epistemic connection between them, therefore, cannot arise—it cannot arise because the 'them' (the two events) are reduced to 'it'.

The Complete Ground—Condition and Conditioned

In order to change a real ground into a complete ground, that is, into a ground that affords the use of the concept of necessity, Hegel introduces the concepts of condition and conditioned. The concept of the conditioned presupposes, of course, the concept of the condition, which itself, therefore, must be unconditioned. The unconditioned cannot be anything but the total system—the system that conditions all finite things.

The *Encyclopaedia* is, on this point, too brief to be of much help. And

---

59. In *Lectures on the History of Philosophy,* Hegel examines in some detail the difference between the aim and method of the Sophists and Plato, respectively; he writes, for instance: "With such reasoning men can easily get so far as to know (where they do not, it is owing to the world of education—but the Sophists were very well educated) that if arguments are relied upon, everything can be proved by argument, and arguments for and against can be found for everything; as particular, however, they throw no light upon the universal, the notion" (Haldane & Simson, tr., *op. cit.,* I, 368).

the *Logic*'s section on complete ground and conditions (*Der vollständige Grund—die Bedingung*) is not only very lengthy but also difficult. In what follows I shall attempt, however, to outline the main points of his arguments and thoughts—without adhering too closely to Hegel's special terminology.

Nature as the Ground of the World—Existence

In the *Logic*, Hegel says that nature is the ground of the world. By "nature" Hegel here understands the laws and the principles that are true of the phenomena of nature (*SL* 464).

Obviously, there is a difference between the laws and principles of nature and the phenomena of nature. Laws are not existential statements; they do not state which phenomena in fact do exist. Built into natural laws is the kind of phenomena to which the laws apply, but there is nothing in the laws that implies the existence of such phenomena. The laws permit inferences from the existence of certain phenomena, where and when they occur, to the existence of other phenomena. But, as Hegel says, the law itself does not bring about the phenomena (*Enz.* §122). Whether a law is not only applicable but in fact applies depends on circumstances governed by other laws. The apples on the tree are governed by the law of gravitation. However, whether apples in fact fall to the ground depends not only on the law of gravitation; it also depends on whether the stem has weakened sufficiently—which again depends on other natural laws. In short, in order that the laws can be applied to something that exists, a system—the totality—of all possible laws is required. This system or totality of all possible laws constitutes the unconditioned condition.[60] In other words, in order to understand that whatever exists does so by necessity requires understanding that it is conditioned by the unconditioned.

It may seem provocative to say that whatever exists does so by necessity. It is acceptable to assert that whatever exists may in one sense or another be derived from the established laws of nature, but it does seem

---

60. "Wenn alle Bedingungen einer Sache vorhanden sind, so tritt sie in die Existenz. Die Sache ist, ehe sie existiert," *Wissenschaft der Logik* (*GW* 11) I, 321. Hegel uses the word "*Sache*," which is a difficult word to translate; both Johnston and Struthers (II, 105) and Miller (*SL* 477) translate it as "fact," so the passage reads: "When all the conditions of a fact are present, it enters into existence. The fact is before it exists." In the present context "fact" is probably the best word for the German word "*Sache*."

provocative to suggest that no other laws of nature are possible. It seems provocative, in other words, to assert that this is the only possible world. When Leibniz said that this world is the best of all possible worlds, it surely implied that other worlds had been possible, although none of them would be as good as the present one. But if we say that this world exists necessarily, we rule out any other possible worlds.

Is it possible to show that a world different from the present one would be a logical impossibility?

If I hit a billiard ball with another billiard ball, the billiard ball I hit will start to roll. And if it does not, there is a reason why it doesn't. This reason must in the last analysis be rooted in our conceptual system, in our categories, or in what has just been called the unconditioned, the totality of conditions. The reason I give if the billiard ball, against expectations, does not begin to roll may be that the impact on the ball was too weak, or maybe that the ball was in some way or other fixed to the billiard table. In other words, I can say that the billiard ball necessarily will start to roll *unless* there is a reason that it should not do it. The reason given must, as mentioned, be rooted in our conceptual or categorial system. If there is nothing that can fill out the 'unless-clause', it must be the case that the ball by necessity will begin to roll.

Suppose, however, that not only am I unable to fill in the 'unless-clause', but I am also able to ascertain that the reason I cannot fill in the unless-clause is the simple one that there is nothing that can satisfy it. How would I describe such a situation? I cannot apply the concept of 'object' to the billiard ball because if it were an object, it would have a mass, and the concept of mass is a physical concept whose meaning is defined in physics. Insofar as the billiard ball is a physical object, it is bound to behave as the physical equations inform us it will behave. I am consequently cut off from all possibilities of describing the situation. Or, to put it differently, I am unable to describe what happened (or, rather, did not happen). And if it is impossible to describe, it is also impossible (i.e., logically impossible) to falsify my expectation of what should have happened. If I expect that a certain state 'S' should occur, then I must of course be able to describe and recognize not only 'S' but also the situation that would falsify 'S.' In order to falsify (or verify) 'S', I must be able to identify that which would falsify it. That which cannot be identified, that is, cannot be conceptualized, cannot be conceived and cannot even be identified, and is therefore a nothing. Obviously, nothing can neither falsify nor verify anything whatsoever.[61] A

---

61. Cf. my article "Knowledge of the Future," *Philosophical Studies* X, no. 6 (1959), 89–96.

condition for not being a nothing, a condition for being either 'S' or 'not S', is that it must be something that has its roots in the categories of thought and consequently in the categories of the laws of nature.

Because nature is an expression of or is rooted in the categories of the absolute, it follows that nature could not be otherwise than it, in fact, is. It means that nature (the laws of nature, the categories) constitutes the unconditioned condition for whatever is.

It is one thing, however, to assert that if there is a nature it must be in accordance with our categories; it is quite another thing to be able to assert that nature exists by necessity. In other words, does Hegel's logic answer the classical metaphysical question: Why is there something and not just nothing?[62]

The answer is, of course, given by what may be regarded as the central thesis of Hegel's philosophy. In the *Phenomenology,* we find the statement (quoted earlier): "In my view, which can be justified only by the exposition of the system itself, everything turns on grasping and expressing the true, not only as *substance*, but equally as *subject*" (*PS* 9–10). And the *Logic* ends by emphasizing the identity between subject and substance or between being and thought. The absolute idea is the unity of the pure concept and its reality. It is, he writes, "contracting itself into the immediacy of *being*, is the *totality* in this form—*nature*" (*SL* 843). In the very last paragraph of the *Encyclopaedia,* it is said briefly and precisely: "We have now returned to the Concept of the Idea with which we began. At the same time this return to the beginning is an advance. What we began with was being, abstract being, while now we have the *Idea* as *being*; and this idea that *is*, is *Nature*" (*Enz.* §244 Addition).

A comparison with Anselm's ontological argument may be of some interest. That argument starts with the concept of a being greater than that which cannot be conceived. From this concept it follows that it must be a concept of a being in reality; because if it were not, we could at least think that it was, in which case it would be greater than the one that was not. The Hegelian dialectical path to the absolute idea begins at the opposite point. It begins with the concept of pure being, the concept that is identical with

---

62. It is noteworthy that in a recent book by Martin Rees, professor of astronomy at Cambridge University, and John Gribbin, an award-winning science writer, it is stated that even if physics should achieve a TOE (a theory of everything), it would not "be the end of physics, or even put all physicists out of work over night. No set of equations explains why there is a universe," *The Stuff of the Universe* (New York: Bantam, 1989), 287f.

nothing; from there, by philosophical analysis of concepts we aim at and end with the absolute idea. Hegel's *Logic* is thus a dialectical move that is just the opposite of the ontological argument. It is the ontological argument upside down. The ontological argument begins with a concept of a being greater than that which cannot (logically cannot) be conceived; the Hegelian system begins with a concept of being purified of every possible attribute, that is, begins with the concept of nothing—a concept which has connotation but no denotation.

A condition for existence is that there is identity between ground and the grounded. If a house is struck by lightning and the house thereby ignites, then one may say (in a sense) that the laws of nature operate in the burning house. What happens in the burning house is a display of the laws of nature.[63]

As we have seen, identity implies difference and difference implies identity. Whatever has existence is accordingly a unity of identity and difference. Whatever exists is therefore related to itself as well as to others; it is an instance of reflection-into-self as well as an instance of reflection-into-other. By uniting reflection-into-self and reflection-into-other, each existent is both self-identical and independent as well as dependent on others. In the preceding example, the burning house is an existent and therefore unites reflection-into-self and reflection-into-other. As a reflection-into-other, it has its ground in the lightning, which itself is both a ground and something to be grounded.[64]

---

63. "Existence, therefore, which is what has emerged from the ground, contains the latter within itself, and the ground does not remain behind existence; instead, it is precisely this process of self-sublation and translation into existence.

"What we have here is therefore also to be found in the ordinary consciousness: when we consider the ground of something, this ground is not something abstractly inward, but is instead itself an existent again. So, for instance, we consider the ground of a conflagration to be a lightning flash that set a building on fire . . ." (*Enz.* §123 Addition). Cf.: "*The fact [Sache] emerges from the ground*. It is not grounded or posited by it in such a manner that ground remains as a substrate; on the contrary, the positing is the movement of the ground outwards to itself and its simple vanishing" (*SL* 477).

64. "Existence is the immediate unity of inward reflection and reflection-into-another. Therefore, it is the indeterminate multitude of existents as inwardly reflected, which are at the same time, and just as much, shining-into-another, or *relational*; and they form a *world* of interdependence and of infinite connectedness of grounds with what is grounded. The grounds are themselves existences, and the existents are also in many ways grounds as well as grounded" (*Enz.* §123).

Things and Properties

As we have just seen, a condition of existence is the unity of reflection–into–self and reflection–into–other. It is a unity that implies that existence is at once both self-sufficient and independent and also dependent on other things. A concept that satisfies this condition is the concept of a thing: The concept of a thing must by necessity involve two concepts: (1) the properties of things, and (2) that which has these properties. Both of these concepts are necessarily united in the concept of a thing. It is deeply engraved in the logic of our language that a thing must have properties (a thing without properties is an abstraction and an ontological absurdity). Likewise, the concept of properties has meaning only as properties of a thing. In the concept of a thing, we use the concept of reflection–into–self; and in the concept of property, we use the concept of reflection–into–other. In the preceding example, the burning house is in itself an individual event. The features and properties that identify the house as a burning house depend on conditions and circumstances outside the house as a reflection–into–self; it depends, among other things, on the lightning; it consequently falls under the concept of reflection–into–other.

The concept of a thing thus conflicts with itself. Both conflicting concepts (the concepts of reflection–into–self and of reflection–into–other) are necessary, and neither of them can be without the other. To understand a thing without properties is an impossibility. We would be left with something like a Kantian "thing in itself." Kant's "thing in itself" is either an obscure concept or a concept bordering on meaninglessness (being either a limiting concept or a concept from which all properties are taken away). Hegel's use of the concept of a "thing in itself" is different. A thing is characterized by its features and properties. The "thing in itself" is the thing before the development of the properties and features that, so to speak, define the thing in question or that constitute its essence. It is the state where these properties and features exist potentially but not yet actually. It is the internal structure that grounds the properties and features of the particular thing.

All things are originally in-themselves. But, as Hegel says, this is not the end of the matter. When a thing in itself has developed into what it should be, it has passed beyond its in-itself and has the properties and features it is supposed to have. As a thing with properties, it now has both reflection–into–self and reflection–into–other.

The difference between the Kantian thing-in-itself (or the Lockean substance) and Hegel's, is that whereas Kant's thing-in-itself and the Lockean substance forever remain beyond all possible knowledge, Hegel's thing-in-itself develops into something fully known. Even as potentially existent, it has its ground in an internal structure; it is knowable (*Enz.* §124 Addition).

In terms of logical grammar we may say that the concept of potential is analyzable by recourse to two concepts: (1) the concept of 'if' (the germ is potentially a plant if the circumstances are right) and (2) the concept of "ground" (the ground for the potential of the germ is the internal structure of the germ).

The relation between a thing and its properties and features, as already mentioned, implies mutually opposed elements: the concept of the thing as reflection-into-self, the thing as the individual and independent unit; and the concept of properties, which expresses the negation of the concept of both the individuality and the independence of the thing. Both of these concepts (the concept of the thing as an independent individual and the concept of the properties) are, once again, necessary. It is a problem, however, to understand the fact that a thing has properties. Hegel has some very interesting remarks about this, although his analysis is impeded by his assumption that properties are definable in terms of matter. It was an assumption shared by the scientists of his day. It was held that to each sense (smell, taste, vision, etc.) corresponds different kinds of matter. In all fairness to Hegel, he saw the difficulties of this assumption and said that they might not be things but only half-things; nevertheless, they are existents (*SL* 492).

Hegel discusses two different expressions we generally use in connection with a thing and its properties. We say that a thing consists of properties. But the expression "consists of" in this connection can be misleading. If I say, for example, that granite consists of such and such minerals, then these minerals can—at least in principle—be separated from that which they constitute. They have their own independent existence. If all the constituents of a thing are taken away, then the thing has disappeared; it has ceased to exist. However, it is logically a different use if I say, for example, that an organism consists of heart, muscles, bones, nerves, and the like. Even though it is, of course, possible to remove all these parts from the organism, if they are removed, they cease to be what they were in the organism. A heart, for instance, is an organ whose function it is to sustain the circulation of the blood. If that function is taken away, it has ceased to be a heart.[65]

With respect to things and properties, the use of "consists of" is neither like the use we have in the example of granite consisting of such and such minerals (the minerals can have an independent existence) nor like the use in the example of an organism consisting of heart, muscles, bones, etc. (removed from the organism, the heart is still a thing though no longer a heart). To conceive of properties as separated from that of which they are properties has no meaning. Obviously, I can scrape the red paint off a piece of wood, but the red stuff scraped away could not with any meaning be identified as the red color as such; whatever is scraped off is bits of wood with red paint.[66] But however we are to understand the concept of 'color', it is certain that we must say that there are colors (cf. *SL* 492). If a man from Mars should ask us whether we here on Earth have red colors, the answer must be affirmative. Obviously it is affirmative because we can point to objects that are red (red flowers, birds with red feathers, etc.). No one would claim that, besides objects that are red, we also have special objects that not only possess the color red but also constitute the very color red itself.

It is no better to say, as we in fact sometimes do say, that a thing *has* this or that property. It is almost impossible not to be logically led astray: The verb 'to have' suggests that there must be a subject, some body that has something or some thing that has or possesses this or that property. This forces us to distinguish two ontological kinds of entities: (1) the thing and (2) its properties. But this distinction violates the logic of both the concept of a thing and the concept of property. It violates the logic of the concept of a thing because it leaves us with a concept of a thing without properties, that is, a Lockean substance or the concept of a Kantian thing-in-itself, both of which are unacceptable. Or it leaves us with a thing that is constituted by, and constituted by nothing but, its properties. In this case, the thing looses its individuality.

An analysis of the concept of a thing in terms of the concept of the in-

---

65. "[T]he various parts or members of the organic body have their subsistence only in their union, and cease to exist as such if they are separated from one another" (*Enz.* §126 Addition).

66. Hegel seems to have difficulties in making up his mind about the logical status of property-words. He remarks: "Indeed the view that things consist of independent stuffs is frequently applied in domains where it has no validity" (*Enz.* §126 Addition).

dividual, independent thing (the reflection-into-self) and the concept of properties (the reflection-into-other) thus cannot succeed. Both concepts are necessary. We cannot do without the concept of the thing as a self-existing entity (reflected-into-self), and the concept of the properties as self-negating plurality (reflecting-into-other). That we cannot do without the concept of property is obvious; we can identify whether a certain object is of a particular kind only through its properties. Properties verify or falsify our assumptions. But we go astray if we go further and claim that the properties *constitute* an object.

We shall now see how Hegel analyzes the concept of a thing without getting involved in the contradictions involved in using the concept of a thing and the concept of its properties.

Appearance

The use of the concept of the object is, as indicated, a necessary condition for consciousness. It is therefore not the existence of objects that is at stake, but the correct analysis of the concept of an object. We have just seen that an analysis in terms of the concepts of 'thing' and 'property' can lead to conflicts. It turns out, however, that an analysis in terms of the concept of appearance avoids those conflicts.

The term 'appearance' is a translation of the German term '*Erscheinung*', a term well known to anyone familiar with Kant's philosophy. Objects appear; nevertheless, it is not correct to say that I see objects. The verb 'to see' is used in the sense of seeing that something is the case. By seeing I ascertain, or try to ascertain, a fact. For example, I see that there is a book on the table, that there is an airplane approaching the airport. But even though it makes good sense to say that by seeing I ascertain a fact (for instance that an airplane is approaching the airport), I most definitely cannot say that I ascertain the airplane. The concept of an object is logically connected to the concept of a fact. Separated or isolated from the concept of a fact, the concept of an object has no meaning. The concept of an object draws its meaning from being logically tied to a fact. If I write with my ballpoint pen on a piece of paper, then I know that I write with my ballpoint pen on a piece of paper. I neither know nor do I not know the ballpoint pen or the piece of paper.[67]

---

67. Cf. my article "On Seeing" (*op. cit.*), or my book *Language and Philosophy* (The Hague & Paris: Mouton, 1972), ch. 4.

Appearance as Law

To say, as I just did, that the concept of an object is logically connected with or tied to the concept of a fact implies that objects are related to other objects. No object exists in a logical vacuum; objects are interrelated. The world of appearance is a world of related objects in which the objects get their meaning from their relation to other objects. It is engraved in the logic of the concept of an object that its meaning is derived from context.

The name by which we identify an object usually indicates the relations that constitute what is meant by the object. For instance, what is a ball? We have billiard balls, footballs, tennis balls, and so on. What we mean, for instance, by a tennis ball can be explained only in terms of its relation to the other objects of the game (such as the net, the racket, and the tennis players). And by a tree we do not mean a description of the elements constituting a tree; what we mean is the relations between the surrounding objects (the soil, the grounds, the air, etc.). Even the most detailed chemical description of, say, a tree would not bring us closer to what we mean by a tree than would a most perfect drawing or painting of it. But if an object is meaning-dependent on other objects, and these other objects in turn are dependent on other objects, then by necessity we end up with a system comprising the totality of all possible objects.

Hegel's concept of appearance is in a conceptually important sense different from Kant's conception. Kant's concept of appearance implies that there is an ontological difference between that which appears and its appearance. According to Hegel, the world itself appears in appearances; in other words, there is no ontological difference between what appears and its appearance. The world of appearance is the essence of the world.[68]

The concept of law is thus central to the essence of appearance. The law constitutes the basis or foundation (*die Grundlage*) of appearance. The law is not outside appearance but is present in it.[69]

---

68. "Law is therefore *essential* appearance" (*SL* 504).

69. "[L]aw is not beyond appearance but is immediately *present* in it . . ." (*SL* 503). Cf. also K.R. Westphal, "Hegel, Philosophy, and Mathematical Physics," *Bulletin of the Hegel Society of Great Britain* 36 (Autumn/Winter 1997), 1–15.

Appearance as Both Reflection-into-Self and Reflection-into-Other

Hegel distinguishes, however, between two kinds of laws. First, there is the law he calls the stable image of the world.[70] The function of this law is to create a unity out of the manifold of sense-experience and to emphasize what is permanent and unchangeable in experience. (Hegel mentions the law of gravity as an example.) The stable image is not distinct from appearance (from the phenomenal world). It is, as just quoted, not outside it but is immediately present in it. Appearance as determined by this aspect of law (the stable image and unity-creating law) Hegel calls the supersensuous world[71]; it constitutes the essential world. This law (or world) is self-identical; it is reflection-into-self.

The other law is determined by reflection-into-other. It is not a kind of law that creates unity or a stable image but a law about the behavior of the objects of sense-experience; that is, it aims at the laws governing the restless flux, a movement from one state of affairs into the opposite.[72]

The Inverted World

These two, reflection-into-self and reflection-into-other, are taken as two different "worlds." Hegel himself speaks, misleadingly, about two worlds. However, what he means is, not that there are two distinct worlds, but that there are two laws applying to one and the same world. The second law states that the selfsame repels itself from itself and is not selfsame but posits itself as selfsame, whereas the first law states that the selfsame remains selfsame. These two laws are plainly opposed. The law (the "world") in which like becomes unlike and unlike becomes like, Hegel terms the inverted (*verkehrte*) law (world) (*SL* 509, cf. *PS* 96–99). According to this law, the positive repels the positive, whereas the positive is identified with the negative (the concept of the positive is determined by the concept of the negative). But neither in the *Phenomenology* nor in the *Logic* does

---

70. "[T]he realm of laws is the *stable* image [*das ruhige Abbild*] of the world of existence or appearance" (*SL* 503).

71. "*Das übersinnliche Welt*" (*SL* 507).

72. "Appearance is the same content but presenting itself in restless flux and as reflection-into-other. It is law as the negative, simply alterable existence, the *movement* of transition into the opposite" (*SL* 504).

Hegel speak of different worlds in any other sense than in the sense of different laws valid for one and the same world of experience.[73] One may, of course, in a metaphysically innocent sense, speak of two different worlds, analogous to the way in which we may say that two different scientific theories within a certain area constitute two different worlds. It is in this sense that we speak of, say, the world of books, the world of mathematics, and the world of music.[74]

---

73. Cf. my *From Radical Empiricism to Absolute Idealism* (*op. cit.*), 128–39. I have also examined the dialectics of the inverted world in my essay "The Inverted World," *Méthexis, Études Néoplatoniciennes, Présentées au Professeur Évanghélos A. Moutsopoulos* (Athens: C.I.E.P.A., 1992), 235–242.

74. "Accordingly, law is not beyond appearance but is immediately *present* in it; the realm of laws is the *stable* image of the world of existence or appearance. But the fact is rather that both form a single totality, and the existent world is itself the realm of laws, which, as that which is simply identical, is also identical with itself in positedness or in the self-dissolving self-subsistence of existence" (*SL* 503). Cf. Hans-Georg Gadamer, "The Inverted World" *The Review of Metaphysics* 28 (1975), 401–422. Without commenting on Gadamer's treatment of the concept of 'the inverted world' in the *Phenomenology*, it seems to me that what he says about it in the version found in the *Logic* corresponds well with my explication here; he says, e.g., "However we read in the *Logic* that law is nothing beyond appearance but rather is directly present in it" (*loc. cit.*, 415). This expresses the fact that the realm of law no longer appears as a (supersensuous) world for "the existing world" is itself the realm of law. Another way to conceive and explain the seemingly absurd statements about the inverted world is to say that Hegel describes it in what the logical positivists (Carnap *et al.*) called the material mode of speech, that is, the mode of speech that has the same form as a language used to speak about things (the so-called 'thing-language'). The seeming absurdities may disappear, however, as I have indicated, by translating them into the formal mode of speech. Hegel's description of the inverted world is in the material mode of speech and is consequently conceived as if he was describing phenomena. If the language of the inverted world is properly translated, it will be seen that it is a description of or rather a prescription for the logical syntax of the concepts of the second law. To say, for instance, that according to the second law a thing, t, is really the opposite of t, is, when properly translated, to say that the rules for using the *concept* of 't' requires the existence of rules for the use of the concept of 'not-t'.

Relation

As we have seen, the world of appearance is determined by two kinds of laws: (1) the stable image whose function is to create a unity among changing phenomena and (2) the laws determining the changes of the world, that is, the laws determining the Heraclitean world.

The category of relation concerns the concepts that constitute the relations among those concepts that come under the unity-creating laws and those that come under the laws for the Heraclitean world. Expressed differently, the categories of relation relate concepts of reflection-into-self and concepts of reflection-into-other. The relevant concepts of relation include those between wholes and parts, force and expression, and inner and outer.

Whole and Parts

The two concepts 'whole' and 'part' are connected by conceptual necessity. It is conceptually impossible to have parts if the parts are not parts of something; and that 'something' of which they are parts is accordingly called the 'whole'. I cut a bread into slices. Each slice is a part of the whole bread. Likewise, to say about something that it is a whole—for instance, the whole bread—implies that it is a whole precisely because it is constituted of parts, namely, the totality of its parts. The whole reflects-into-self, whereas the parts reflect-into-other. As reflecting-into-other, the parts are identical with appearances.

We do not talk about wholes unless it means a whole constituted by parts. Consequently, we do not call a grain of salt or a pen a whole. The simple reason is that we do not cut either a grain of salt or a pen into pieces. But a bread or a layer cake is (normally) meant to be divided into pieces; either of them may be said to constitute a whole. The person selling bread or layer cakes may ask the buyer whether she or he wants the whole bread or maybe only half of it, or ask whether she or he wants only a slice of the layer cake.

Although we have been talking of concrete (extant) objects such as slices of bread or pieces of layer cake, Hegel's point is not about the laws governing the behavior of such objects. His point is to reveal the logical behavior (the logical grammar or, if one prefers, the depth grammar) of the concepts of 'whole' and 'part'. Hegel's result is that the two concepts imply each other. In a certain sense, therefore, they are identical. That is, they have the same denotation, but surely different connotation. Indeed, their connotations are mutually opposed, but neither concept can be used alone; they must be used together.[75]

Let us note that there is a (logical) difference between the relations of the whole and its parts, and the relations of a whole and its constituents. The former is between a bread and its slices. The totality of slices makes up the bread, just as the pieces of layer cake make up the layer cake. However, the bread is not made of slices, but rather consists of flour and yeast and other ingredients, just as the layer cake consists of flour, cream, and (maybe) chocolate. A machine is not a whole; it cannot be divided into parts; there cannot be slices of a machine. But a machine consists of different materials (for instance steel or iron). The different parts that compose a machine imply a relation between physical objects; this is thus an empirical (a nonlogical) relation. The relation, however, between a whole and its parts (such as the bread and the slices) is a nonempirical, logical relation. Because the logical relation holds between concepts, and not between physical objects, it has no meaning to say that the whole consists of concepts! A machine consists of steel or iron; it does not consist of concepts.

Because the concepts of wholes and parts imply each other, it follows, as we have seen, that we cannot use either of those concepts without presupposing the other. Forgetting this results in the age-old problem of infinite divisibility, according to which the concept of a whole implies an entity that is already divided into parts.[76] Such parts lose their logical

75. Cf. Hegel's remark: "*The whole is equal to the parts and the parts to the whole. There is nothing in the whole which is not in the parts, and nothing in the parts which is not in the whole*" (*SL* 515).

76. "The whole and the parts therefore *condition* each other; but the relation here considered is at the same time higher than the relation of *conditioned* and *condition* to each other. . . . Here this relation is *realized*, that is, it is *posited* that condition is the essential self-subsistence of the conditioned in such a manner that it is *presupposed* by the latter" (*SL* 515).

status as "part" the moment the part itself is divided; its logical status has changed from being a part to being a whole. In other words, to speak about a part being divided into other parts that are themselves divided into still other parts—in other words, to speak about parts' divisibility—is to commit a conceptual error.

To repeat, the relation between a whole and its parts is a relation between two identical concepts as far as denotation is concerned. But as far as connotation is concerned, it is a relation between two different, indeed opposed, concepts. In the former case, the relation is a reflection-into-self, whereas in the latter case, the relation is a reflection-into-other. The relation between wholes and parts is thus a relation where a reflection-into-self implies a reflection-into-other and *vice versa;* it is a relation where a reflection-into-other implies a reflection-into-self.

Force and Expression

The concept of a force is a concept of something individual that, all the same, implies the concept of a plurality of expressions or manifestations. A force manifests itself in a plurality of phenomena. These phenomena, as phenomena, occur in a law-governed way. They come into and go out of existence. They go out of existence and, as Hegel says, back into their ground.[77]

Talking about "force and its expression" seems clearly to imply that we are talking about two ontological entities: the force itself and its manifestations or expressions. Hegel emphasizes instead that the force is identical to its expressions; the word 'force' and the words 'the expression of the force' have the same denotation although they have different connotations. A force that does not express itself is simply not a force. To say that a force is an ontological entity different from its expressions deprives the word 'force' of any denotation; or rather, if it is supposed to refer to anything at all, it will forever remain an unknown entity (cf. *Enz.* §136 and Addition).

If there is no difference between a force and its expression, then it has no meaning to say that the force is the "cause" of the expression of the force. Saying that the force causes its expressions would be the same as saying that the force caused itself. However, the following two statements do not contradict each other:

---

77. "[F]orce passes over into *its expression*, and what is expressed is a vanishing something which withdraws into force as into its ground; it *is*, only as borne and posited by force" (*SL* 519).

1. A force is not a cause of its expressions.

2. There is a cause of the fact that a force expresses itself.

Take as an example a piece of magnetic iron that attracts some iron filings. We describe this phenomenon—and do so correctly—by saying that, because of its magnetism, the piece of iron attracts the iron filings. It would be a misunderstanding, however, to take this to mean that the magnetism of the piece of iron is the cause of the movements of the iron filings toward the magnetic iron. The logical place of magnetism in the explanation of the movement of the iron filings is not to function as a cause, but to function as a law-concept. To say that something is magnetic is to say that, if objects of a certain kind of material and weight are placed at a certain distance from a magnetic piece of metal, then those objects move toward the magnet.

The cause of the phenomenon of attraction is the placing of the magnetic piece and the iron filings at a proper distance from each other. The cause, in other words, is whatever circumstances occasion the law of magnetism to apply. The law of magnetism can be expressed as a conditional statement of the form 'if . . ., then . . .'. The events or circumstances that constitute the cause or causes are ones whose descriptions are to be filled in after the 'if'; these are the "initial conditions" in a causal explanation.

In his analysis of the phenomenon of attraction (i.e., what happens the moment the force manifests itself—when for instance a magnet attracts some iron filings), Hegel uses the concept of solicitation (*Sollizitieren*). Hegel uses this concept as follows: If instead of some iron filings I place a small piece of wood in front of the magnet, nothing happens. The difference between the piece of wood and the iron filings is that the iron filings are able to solicit the magnet to manifest itself, something a piece of wood cannot do. However, not only do the filings solicit the magnet to attract the filings, the filings solicit the magnet to solicit the filings to solicit the magnet.

To express this generally: Suppose force A solicits B to solicit A, then A solicits B to behave as it ought to insofar as some law L applies to B. A solicits B to solicit A to solicit B.[78]

---

78. "Or it solicits only in so far as it is solicited to solicit. And so, conversely, the first force is solicited only in so far as it itself solicits the other to solicit it, namely the first force. Each of the two therefore receives the impulse from the other; but the impulse which it gives as active force consists in its receiving an impulse from the other; the impulse which it receives was solicited by itself" (*SL* 522).

This sounds circular, but it is not a vicious circle. Consider again the magnet and the iron filings: The magnet solicits the filings to be attracted. In order that the magnet should be capable of soliciting the filings, it must itself be solicited—solicited namely by the filings. So the filings start the process by soliciting the magnet to solicit the filings. That is, as I just said, not a vicious circle; it would be vicious only if the verb 'to solicit' entailed 'to be solicited to solicit'. The process of solicitation can begin only if the circumstances are right (that is, if the circumstances constitute a cause; being the right kind of metal located at the right range of distance from the magnet). Likewise, this process is terminated by the fact that the filings are actually attracted.

It is important, however, to understand that when Hegel speaks about solicitation he is not speaking about happenings occurring in time. Hegel does not describe phenomena of attraction, nor does he attempt to explain them. What Hegel does is to emphasize that the concept of force must be conceived as two mutually opposing concepts: passivity and activity. These two concepts neutralize each other.

Outer and Inner

If the active concept (i.e., the concept of soliciting) is an expression of the 'inner', and the passive concept (the concept of being solicited) is an expression of the 'outer', then their difference reduces to nothing. Because the force (the active and inner) is identical with its expressions (the passive and outer), this entails that the two concepts 'inner' and 'outer' do not apply in such contexts. In ordinary contexts, the two words are of course necessary: My car is not in the garage, it is parked outside in the street; my furniture is inside the house. Indeed, there are expressions of force associated with the magnet that occur inside the magnet and there are expressions that occur outside it. In other words, to say that the two concepts 'inner' and 'outer' are identical and, therefore, cannot be applied, is true insofar as their alleged metaphysical use is concerned, although it would be absurd to deny that these concepts have a use within ordinary language. In fact they are necessary conditions for the use of any such language. The Sun, for instance, is necessarily a source of energy. A great many processes (a great many expressions of energy) take place inside the Sun, and a great many expressions of that force take place outside the Sun. The concepts 'inner' and 'outer' are here used as they are normally used in ordinary language. But in their metaphysical use, they cancel each other. To speak of 'inner' and 'outer' in that sense, if it could mean anything at all, would

mean something like this: There are some processes that cannot be classified as expressions of force, but only as its cause or source. This would imply that one and the same process would be both active and passive and
consequently would be impossible; neither concept would be (in this case)
inapplicable.

That the concepts of inner and outer are inapplicable in metaphysical
contexts does not imply that everything is either inner or outer. There can
be an inner only where there also is an outer and vice versa. But because
both concepts (in metaphysical contexts) are inapplicable, it means that
nothing is either or. Dualism (such as Cartesian dualism) is therefore, according to Hegel, an untenable view. It is consequently not possible, Hegel
maintains, to distinguish a person's character from his acts. A person's
character and ethical worth are identical with his or her acts—although
Hegel (like Kant) admits that there are cases where the motive is to act in a
correct way, but nevertheless, because of circumstances, things turn out
quite differently from what was intended—in which case the ethical value
of the act is unaffected. In general, however, Hegel holds that a person is
identical with his or her acts. It is an expression of envy, Hegel claims,
when a great person's acts are denigrated by ascribing "base" motives
to them.[79]

---

79. Here Hegel deserves to be quoted: ". . . it is also very often the case that in
judging others, who have brought about something fair, square, and solid, we may
employ the false distinction of inward and outward, in order to maintain that what
they have done is only something external to them, and that their inner motives
were completely different, because they acted to satisfy their vanity or some other
discreditable passion. This is the envious disposition which, being itself unable to
accomplish anything great, strives to drag greatness down to its own level and to
belittle it. As against this, we may recall the fine saying of Goethe, that for the great
superiorities of others there is no remedy but love. So if in order to depreciate the
praiseworthy achievements of others there is talk of hypocrisy, we must notice, on
the contrary, that although a man may certainly dissemble and hide a good deal in
single instances, still he cannot hide his inner self altogether; it reveals itself infalli-
bly in the *decursus vitae* [course of life], so that even in this connection it must be
said that a man is nothing but the series of his acts" (*Enz.* §140 Addition).

Actuality

The categories of essence, as we have seen, are double: essence and appearance. Essence is the inner (reflection-into-self) and appearance is the outer (reflection-into-other). The unity of essence and appearance—the unity of inner and outer—constitutes the category of actuality. The concept of actuality is, consequently, a concept neither of the inner nor of the outer; this is so because, as we have seen, the inner and the outer are identical (the essence of an object is identical with its appearance).[80] To say that the inner and the outer are identical is to say that the two expressions have the same denotation—they have the same reference and must be used conjointly, although they have different, opposed connotations. Precisely because the concepts inner and outer have the same denotation but not the same connotation, in their unity the distinction between them is not obliterated; it is preserved—it is sublated.

Actuality and Reason

One of Hegel's famous statements is this: "What is rational is actual and what is actual is rational."[81] Hegel considers this statement to be fundamental for all philosophy. On this statement "the plain man like the

---

80. The point of the *Phenomenology* is to demonstrate that there is identity between subject and object (cf. *PS* 9). And in the *Logic*, as mentioned earlier in the section on categories of being-for-self, Hegel declares that the fact that the finite can be understood only through true infinity proves the truth of idealism (cf. *SL* 154–56).

81. "Vorrede," *Philosophie des Rechts*, here quoted from T. M. Knox's translation, *Hegel's Philosophy of Right* (Oxford: Oxford University Press, 1952), 10; cf. *Enz.* §6.

philosopher takes his stand, and from it philosophy starts in its study of the universe of mind as well as the universe of nature."[82] Those who are acquainted with German idealism—that is, the philosophy that reached its apex with Hegel's philosophy—will know that this statement forms the basis of German idealism. If we cut away all the psychological elements—elements that as merely psychological are irrelevant to conceptual logic—we are led by conceptual necessity from Kant's transcendental apperception, through Fichte's universal ego and Schelling's universal reason, to Hegel's assertion that "everything turns on grasping and expressing the true not only as substance but equally as subject" (*PS* 9–10).[83] The subject Hegel speaks of here is the universal subject or universal reason.[84] To investigate the logical structure of universal reason is precisely the task for Hegel's successor for Kant's transcendental logic, namely, what Hegel calls speculative logic.[85]

Modality: Possibility, Contingency, and Necessity

Actuality is the scene of changes. Some changes can be ruled out because they are simply impossible. That water at 100°C should change into ice instead of boiling is impossible; a fluid that behaved in such a way would not be water. It would be a contradiction to assume that it could be. We do not need to verify this empirically; or rather, neither verification nor falsification would be possible, just because whatever we would observe, no observation could count as water changing into ice at 100°C; we could not then regard it as water!

The situation is different with contingent changes. They are changes that can occur; they cannot be ruled out of bounds. A meteorologist

---

82. *Philosophy of Right* (*op. cit.*), p. 10.

83. In my book, *From Radical Empiricism to Absolute Idealism* (*op. cit.*), I have analyzed in detail the conceptual development from Kant's transcendental apperception to Hegel's absolute.

84. The expression 'universal reason' is in fact redundant. The concept of reason implies necessity, which of course implies universality. The concept of reason is consequently not a psychological (or empirical) concept.

85. This seems to imply a circle. Reality is identical with reason. One of the categories of reason is reality. But to say that one of the categories of reason is reality is, then, to say that one of the categories of reality is reality. In order to avoid this circularity one may say that reality is a meta-concept, that is, logic has to discover the categories of reality; among these categories reality cannot figure.

predicts rain tomorrow. Rain is therefore likely; that is, it is possible that it will rain. If this prediction turns out false, we might think that the meteorologist is not as reliable as he ought to be. But being a bad meteorologist is still to be a meteorologist. We do not define a meteorologist as a person whose predictions of the weather necessarily must come true. The fact, however, that we may say that a meteorologist may be a bad meteorologist (i.e., that her or his predictions are not always reliable) implies that there could be meteorologists whose predictions were always true. This is to say that it is possible to make only true predictions provided one knows all the facts and all the meteorological laws. If this were the case, then the predictions could be made with certainty. Meteorological changes occur with necessity from preceding weather conditions and the various laws of meteorology.

This kind of possibility, the possibility of rain, is thus based on the possibility that the meteorologist is not an omniscient meteorologist. It is not the case that changes that actually occur in the weather do not occur with necessity according to the laws of meteorology.

As an example of something that is indeed utterly unlikely but not logically impossible, Hegel notes that it is possible that the sultan could be appointed a pope (*Enz.* §143 Addition). In order to say that this is logically possible, one must be able to describe coherently the conditions that would satisfy such an appointment: The sultan must first convert to Catholicism; he must then turn out to be an outstanding member of the Catholic hierarchy; he must not only be educated theologically but also be appointed a cardinal, etc., etc. All of this is, of course, so utterly unlikely that it can be disregarded as a possibility, despite the fact that there is no contradiction involved in the statement that circumstances could develop in such a way that the sultan may become a pope.

It might be suggested that a person's behavior, in this case the sultan's conversion to Catholicism, happens according to psychological laws; although we may not have sufficient knowledge of the psychological circumstances and the applicable psychological laws—sufficient to be able to predict how a person, in this case the sultan, by necessity will behave—his behavior is nevertheless law-governed. However, as far as the present example is concerned, there are so many circumstances that must be satisfied that it is at least debatable whether it is, even in principle, predictable that the sultan could be elected as pope.

Another of Hegel's examples of an event that he classifies as a logical possibility (which means that its denial would be a necessary falsehood) cannot be accepted. "It is possible," Hegel writes, "that the Moon might fall upon the Earth tonight." In other words, the statement: "It is impossible that the Moon might fall upon the Earth tonight," according to Hegel, is a false statement. Hegel denied that this statement is true by necessity, although in fact it is. The Moon is an astronomical object, and as such it is determined by the relevant astronomical theory. According not only to astronomy, but also to physics and all other relevant sciences, the Moon simply cannot fall upon the Earth tonight. If by the word 'Moon' one understands nothing but a visual sense-datum (which, of course, one cannot), only a minimum of theories and predictions, if any at all, could be associated with it. But if today "the Moon" behaves contrary to what our scientific theories maintain, it would be impossible even to say what in fact we did observe. One could not say it was the Moon because what we mean by the Moon is an astronomical object to which the concepts of mass and inertia necessarily apply and, consequently, must behave according to the laws defining those concepts.

The natural sciences are subject to change: they falsify, correct, and improve their theories. However, if the fundamental concepts of science as such are suspended, one cannot even describe what happens. One is deprived of the very conditions of having a language.[86] And without a language, one can neither think nor even observe.[87] By the concept of 'the Moon' (that is, the Earth's satellite) one can understand only what the various relevant sciences have ascertained; consequently one cannot accept other kinds of behavior than those prescribed by established theories.

As mentioned, Hegel asserts that the actual is rational. Curiously, in the *Logic* Hegel states that we can imagine phenomena or rather describe such imagined phenomena that, so he claims, can be classified as contingent. These descriptions are statements that can be denied without contradiction—the contradiction, for instance, that the Moon is not the Moon! But as we have just seen, this is not the case.

Hegel's result is that the concept of possibility is a psychological concept only. "Possibility" indicates that one is incapable of determining whether something or other will in fact be the case: "It is possible that it will be raining tomorrow"; "He may possibly become just as tall as his father"; "Cardinal so-and-so may possibly become the next pope"; "There is a good chance that he will recuperate fully." The concept is not used to say that there could be events that do not occur with necessity.

This goes against what logical positivism taught: All sentences are either tautological or contingent. In Carnap's famous essay "Testability and

---

86. Cf. my article "Knowledge of the Future" (*op. cit.*).
87. Cf. my article "On Seeing" (*op. cit.*).

Meaning" he states, for instance, that a sentence like "Rivers flow up-hill" is a contingent statement. It is a statement that is verifiable.[88] Hegel's point is that this cannot be. If I find a river that flows up-hill, I am not verifying the statement that rivers flow up-hill. I shall be puzzled indeed—and I shall remain so until I have found an acceptable explanation, an explanation that accords with our scientific theories. This case parallels Hegel's statement about the Moon falling upon the Earth tonight. The difference between Carnap and Hegel here is this: For Carnap to say what he does is wrong, but it accords with the philosophy of logical positivism; Hegel's example that the Moon could fall upon the Earth is a bad example. It is a bad example in the sense that it runs counter to his theory of necessity (which is a correct theory); it runs counter to his statement that "What is rational is actual and what is actual is rational."

In fact, most cases commonly classified as logically possible are just the opposite: they are logically impossible. They are logically impossible in the sense that the case or the event said to be logically possible would violate the logical grammar of the concepts involved: The falling Moon could not be the Moon; the water flowing up-hill could not be water, etc. The difference between 'logically possible' and 'possible' is thus that the former (for instance, the Moon is falling) is not possible; it is in fact logically impossible, whereas the latter (for instance, that it is going to rain tomorrow) is possible in the sense that, as far as our knowledge goes, it may become the case; although if it turns out to be true, it is so by necessity.

It may be objected that I am forgetting the principle of the indeterminacy associated with Heisenberg's name. An alleged entity of quantum mechanics can never at one and the same time possess an exact position and an exact velocity. Although Heisenberg's principle of indeterminism presupposed the theories of such physicists as Max Planck, Niels Bohr, and Erwin Schrödinger and much more mathematics than it would be possible to discuss here, it is interesting that already the ancient Greek thinkers (as well as Hegel) were aware of problems in connection with the concept of movement. They were problems which as Hegel expresses it "the ancient dialecticians saw."[89] I explained earlier how it is logically

---

88. Carnap, in agreement with Moritz Schlick, writes: "Thus he [Schlick] thinks, e.g., that the sentence S': 'Rivers flow up-hill,' is verifiable, because it is logically possible that rivers flow up-hill. I agree with him that this fact is logically possible and that the sentence S', mentioned above, is verifiable," "Testability and Meaning" (*Philosophy of Science* 3, 1936, 419–71), 423.

89. Cf. note 53.

impossible to determine the exact position of an object, however small, which moves continuously.[90] The greater velocity the object or entity has, the greater is the indeterminacy of its place. To decrease the degree of indeterminacy of its place at a certain moment, it is necessary to decrease its velocity. It is part of the meaning of the concept of movement that if x moves, then if x at a certain moment is at the point p, then x is not at that very same moment at p. Or in other words, the logic of our language cannot apply to the movement of infinitely small points, since that would entail that any such point both is and is not at a certain infinitely small point in space.

It is easy in this connection to make a conceptual error. We talk about infinitely small objects, entities, or even points in space and talk about infinitely short durations of time—an 'instant', a 'now'. We may then be led to take a radical but fatal step, namely this: We change the points in space into geometrical points and 'the nows' into instants without duration, that is, into "geometrical" points of time. A geometrical point does not constitute even the smallest possible unit of space; because it has no extension, it is not a point in space at all; and just as little is a geometrical point in time an instant of time at all. The consequence of taking this step is that the problems connected with continuous movement cannot arise. Geometrical points do not move in space; they are not in space at all; they cannot with any meaning be said to have or not to have a spatial position at any 'now' because the now as an instant without duration is not a part of time.[91] Of course, when we are dealing with objects of experience, it is obviously false to say that a moving object cannot at one and the same moment have both an exact velocity and an exact position. If I drive my car through a certain village, it is absolutely true that I 'now' am in that village, where the 'now' may extend over several minutes. If I walk through the rooms of a rather large apartment, it is equally true that at any time during the walk I can answer the question: "Where are you right now?" I can truly answer, "Right now I am in the dining room" or "Right now I am in the living room." In other words, it is only within quantum mechanics that the principle of indeterminacy applies. If we take the logical leap to geometrical points, then

90. Cf. pp. 29–31, 48–49 above; see also "Movements, Moments, and Beginning" (*op. cit.*).

91. I have traced some of the conceptual problems that arise from failing to distinguish between infinitely small extensions and geometrical points, and between instants with infinitely small duration and instants with no duration whatever in my article, "Movements, Moments, and Beginning" (*op. cit.*)

the principle negates itself. And if we are dealing with objects of experience, then it is plainly false.

We may thus conclude that the principle of indeterminacy has no bearing on the concept of necessity that Hegel claims to be essential to the concept of actuality as he expresses it in his famous statement: "What is rational is actual and what is actual is rational."

The point of these remarks is that when we deal with a "fallen Moon" or with "rivers flowing up-hill" we are dealing with natural laws and phenomena whose truth is unaffected by the "ancient dialecticians'" insight or Heisenberg's principle of indeterminacy based, as it is, on advanced mathematics.

Absolute Relations

For clarity, I reiterate: The rational is the actual and the actual is the rational; differently expressed: The real, which as we have seen, is identical with appearances, is what possesses necessity. Three kinds of relations determine the structure of appearances: (1) substance and accident, (2) cause and effect, and (3) reciprocity.

Substance and Accident

Because reality and appearance are one and the same thing, and reality is unconditioned (if it were not it would be conditioned by what is unreal, which of course would be absurd), it follows that reality has its ground in itself. That which has its ground in itself and is understood by itself is called substance. This conception of substance is in some sense closely related to Spinoza's view, but differs from Descartes's view. The Cartesian view is determined by the necessity of preserving the identity of an object undergoing change. The piece of wax that continually undergoes changes while being heated is nevertheless one and the same piece of wax, even though whatever can be observed constantly changes. Nothing empirical can therefore constitute its identity. Consequently, its identity is constituted by a nonempirical substance. The properties or attributes of the substance change, although the substance which has those properties does not.

Hegel speaks of substance and its accidents. What is the relation between a substance and its accidents? In the *Encyclopaedia*, Hegel writes: "Substance . . . is the totality of the accidents; it reveals itself in them as their absolute negativity, i.e., as the *absolute might* and at the same time as the *richness of all content*" (§151). In other words, substance is absolute power. The question, therefore, is how are we to understand 'power' in this connection? The power Hegel has in mind is "the tremendous power of the negative" (*PS* 19). The power of negation is the power that explains the appearance and disappearance of accidents. Accidents constitute the ever-changing world, the Heraclitean world. In this world everything comes into being and goes out of being and at no time remains unchanged. To conceive substance as power is to conceive it as the ground of whatever is and of what explains it. And to associate power with negation is to conceive power as that which ultimately explains the ever-changing world of accidents—the world in which everything appears, only in the next moment to be destroyed. If A is succeeded by B which in turn is succeeded by C, it follows that the appearance of B means the destruction of A, and the appearance of C is the destruction of B.[92] The concept of power is thus, in this connection, to be understood epistemologically and metaphysically.

As mentioned earlier, Hegel's concept of substance has some affinity with Spinoza's. To both Spinoza and Hegel, substance is a unity because everything is connected by law; everything is connected not only in fact but by necessity. Spinoza characterizes substance as creative or active nature (*natura naturans*); it is through creative or active nature that everything else, namely created or passive nature (*natura naturata*), exists and is conceived.

Active nature is often thought to be the ultimate cause of passive nature. This is a misconception. Active or creative nature is as little the cause of passive or created nature as Hegel's substance is the cause of its accidents.[93] Neither Spinoza's active nature nor Hegel's substance are special ontological entities, which they would have to be if they had the logical status of a cause. One may say that they both, in a certain sense, are *in* passive nature or *in* the accidents, respectively. There are no other ontological entities than created or passive nature or accidents.

The concept of substance is an expression of reflection-into-self (a substance exists by itself and is understood by itself). Through "the tremendous power of negativity," it is transformed into its 'other', that is, accidents, which accordingly are classified as reflection-into-other. Although

---

92. "Substance manifests itself through actuality with its content into which it translates the possible, as *creative* power and through the possibility to which it reduces the actual, as *destructive* power. But the two are identical, the creation is destructive and the destruction is creative; for the negative and the positive, possibility and actuality unite in substantial necessity" (*SL* 556).

93. Concerning Spinoza's concept of substance, see my *History of Philosophy* (*op. cit.*), 96–104.

Hegel's substance neither is nor could be a cause, he nevertheless sometimes writes as if it were a cause. In the *Encyclopaedia*, he writes: "Substance is *cause*, because—in contrast to its passing-over into accidentality—it is inwardly reflected; and in this way, it is the *originating Thing* [*Sache*]. But it is cause also because it equally sublates the inward reflection (or its mere possibility); i.e., because it posits itself as the negative of itself, and in that way produces an *effect*: an actuality which is therefore only a *posited* one, although at the same time it is a necessary one in virtue of the causal process" (§153).

It seems as if Hegel states here explicitly that substance is that which causes accidents. Nevertheless, this is hardly what Hegel means. As Crawford Elder notes, "Hegel not infrequently uses language of physical alteration to express conceptual entailments."[94] When Hegel says that substance is "the originating Thing" (*die ursprungliche Sache*) it is obvious that he does not mean (cannot mean) that substance is a thing. What he does mean is that the concept of substance is required for the understanding of accidents. The very use of the word 'accident' has meaning only under the conditions of the concept of substance. But to say that the concept of substance is a presupposition for the concept of accidents, of course, rules out any causal connection between them. A concept cannot meaningfully count as a cause.

Accidents are "forces, which require solicitation from one another and have one another for condition" (*SL* 556). Accidents stand in a mutual causal relation. But, obviously, what effects a cause may have depends on a law that determines the nature of the causal relationship. And this is in fact what Hegel holds: "In so far as such an accidental seems to exercise power over another, it is the power of substance which embraces both within itself" (*SL* 556–57). In other words, take away the law, and accidents cannot be causes. The law (the substance) is the reason (misleadingly: the 'cause') that accidents are causes. Substance both enables and requires that accidents generate whatever causal relations they have.

The relation between a substance and its accidents differs from the relation between, say, a force and its expressions. A force, e.g., magnetism, requires an object that is magnetic. For a magnetic force to manifest itself requires objects that constitute those manifestations. There must be two (or more) different objects: That which manifests the force and, secondly, the manifestations. The manifestations require that of which they are a manifestation. To the question "Of what are they manifestations?" the

---

94. *Op. cit.*, 5.

answer cannot be "the manifestations are manifestations of themselves." That would be like demonstrators in the street, who, when asked what they protest, answered, "We protest this demonstration." In the relation between a substance and its accidents, there are not, and cannot be, more than one ontological entity. To conceive it as substance is to conceive it as accidents, and to conceive it as accidents is to conceive it as substance.

Causality

According to traditional views, the concept of causality involves two events or occurrences. One event is the cause, whereas the other, which follows immediately upon the first, is the effect. Because of its fundamental epistemological role, it has been extremely important to safeguard the validity of the concept of causation—especially after the almost deadly blow David Hume delivered it. As Hume argued, there is not, in fact cannot be, any necessary link between the event we regard as the cause and the event we regard as the effect. From the event we regard as the cause, we have no right to infer that the event we regard as the effect must take place. Such inferences—which we not only do, but must make (all our behavior is based on such inferences)—cannot be epistemologically justified, but only psychologically explained (according to Hume). Kant thought he could safeguard causality by making it an *a priori* concept that has its roots in the objective *a priori* time sequence (the ship flowing downstream) in contrast to the subjective time sequence (whether I observe a house by starting from the roof and ending at the ground, or have the sequence reversed, starting with the ground and ending at the roof, is a sequence which rests on my choice; this sequence is decided by the subject.)[95]

Hegel's approach is entirely different. Hegel denies that the concept of causality implies two events. If causality thus involves the occurrence of not two but only one event, then the problem of the necessary connection,

---

95. That substance is not a cause is clearly expressed by Kuno Fischer in his famous *Hegels Leben, Werke und Lehre*: "Substance is not, properly speaking, the productive, but rather just the destructive power of things; it doesn't posit things, rather, it presupposes their existence and makes them into accidents; it reveals or manifests itself in their nullity" (*op. cit.*), 522. For Hume's and Kant's views of causality, see my *History of Philosophy* (*op. cit.*), 151–162, 169–195, respectively; for further details, see my *Kant's Theory of Knowledge* (New York: Harcourt, Brace & World, 1965).

or lack of necessary connection, between the allegedly separate events cannot even arise.[96]

Hegel argues as follows: A cause is a cause only at the moment it produces its effect, and an effect is an effect only the moment it is produced as an effect—which is the very same moment the cause causes it. Moreover, at the very moment the cause causes the effect, the cause loses its status as a cause. If I turn the light on by flipping the switch, my flipping the switch is the cause, but after the light is on, it has no meaning to say that my flipping the switch still is the cause. It *was* the cause of the light going on, but it is not the cause of the fact that it still is on. It ceases as a cause the moment it causes the effect. Likewise, the moment the cause causes the effect, the effect stops being an effect. The fact that the light is on is explained as an electrical phenomenon. It is explained by electrical concepts, not by the action of the person who turned the switch on. The cancer patient's disease is described in medical terms; it is not described as an effect of, say, too much smoking or some other features of his lifestyle.[97]

This entails two important points: First, it is a conceptual error to conceive of cause and effect as two events instead of only one; second, it entails that the usual view of causality, as a transition from the cause to the effect (i.e., as a process) is a conceptual error. There is no time gap between the occurrence of the cause and the occurrence of the effect. Causality is thus threatened by a paradox connected with the concept of 'now': At the very moment it is correct to say 'now', it is also correct that the 'now' already has passed.[98] In other words, at the 'now' in which the cause produces its effect, that now has already passed. This implies that the cause is both a cause and is not a cause, and that the effect is both an effect and is not an effect. Because Hegel does discuss the paradox in this connection, it may suffice to quote Hegel's remark about the paradox of motion: That which moves is at any moment both 'here' and 'not here'. This does not

---

96. That a cause and its effect do not constitute two events, but only constitute one event, I have argued in "Some Remarks on Causality," *The Journal of Philosophy* L no. 15 (1953), 466–71.

97. "Cause is cause only insofar as it produces an effect, and cause is nothing but this determination, to have an effect, and effect is nothing but this, to have a cause. Cause as such implies its effect, and effect implies cause; insofar as cause has not yet acted, or it has ceased to act, then it is not cause, and effect insofar as its cause has vanished, is no longer effect but an indifferent actuality" (*SL* 559).

98. Cf. Hegel's discussion of the law of contradiction (*SL* 440).

mean, Hegel writes, "that therefore there is no motion, but on the contrary, that motion is *existent* contradiction itself" (*SL* 440).

Nevertheless, there is good reason to conceive of causality as a process involving two events where the cause occurs before the effect. Suppose I put my finger into some water with the inevitable result that the finger gets wet. Before the finger is put into the water, there is still no cause–effect relation. However, the moment I put my finger into the water, the effect occurs. Nevertheless, it serves a purpose to call the event of 'putting my finger into the water'—an event describable as part of my behavior, and consequently a temporal process—the cause. By describing the cause as my behavior, I have truly given an explanation of why my finger is wet.[99] However, this does not change the conceptual fact that neither the cause nor the effect is a process. Neither the cause *qua* cause, nor the effect *qua* effect, has any conceptual content; neither can be described as such, independently of the other.[100]

Reciprocity

As we have just seen, a cause is a cause only at the very moment that it creates the effect. Thus, being a cause depends on creating an effect. The effect is thus in a sense a cause of the cause being a cause. This implies that the cause is a cause of its effect, at the same time as this very effect is the cause of the cause which causes it. In other words, every cause is both a cause and its effect, and every effect is both an effect and its cause. However, although cause and effect thus turn out to be identical, they are identical only in the sense of having the same denotation; obviously, they have different connotations. And yet, what meaning can be given to a moment without duration, that is, the moment that constitutes the common denotation of cause and effect? As noted earlier, when he dealt with Zeno's paradox, Hegel rightly maintained that a line could be measured by help of

---

99. In "The Language of Causality" (*Dialogos* 11, 1977, 7–21), I have argued that the necessity of the cause–effect relationship is the result of the use of what could be characterized as causal verbs; they are verbs like 'to push,' 'to cut,' 'to ignite,' 'to make wet'. To push is to have pushed, to cut is to have cut, to ignite is to have ignited, to make wet is to have made wet, etc.

100. "But the true point is that we cannot even draw a conceptual distinction between 'effect as it is in itself', and 'effect as it stands towards its cause', or between 'cause as it is in itself', and 'cause as it is towards its effect'," Crawford Elder, *Appropriating Hegel* (*op. cit.*), 26.

units like centimeters, meters, and the like. In a sense, a distance consists of such units, but it is a conceptual error to say that it consists of points. (It has no meaning to say that a certain distance measures so many points!) Likewise, a certain period of time in a sense consists of so many time units, such as seconds, minutes, and hours, and is measured in terms of these units. But because an instantaneous 'now' or a durationless 'moment' is not a unit of time, no period consists of so many moments, and no length of time can be measured in terms of moments. If we use the term 'now' or the term 'moment' to indicate a certain extremely short period of time, that period is measurable in time-units such as a fraction of a second, and there is no limit to the brevity of the moment. Indeed, this brief moment also cannot consist of durationless moments, no more than a distance can be said to consist of points.

The fact that these two concepts—concepts that constitute 'the cement of the world'—not only imply each other, but are each other's cause and each other's effect, expresses reciprocity. There is no cause whose effect is not at the same time also the cause of the cause of which it is the effect.

Recall that the concept of causation is tied to the concept of substance—not as the concept of substance in itself, that is, as a reflection-into-self, but as a reflection-into-other. Causality is thus tied to accidents—accidents that are what they are because they are determined by substance; they are determined by the law (or laws) that is (or are) the essence of the substance. Therefore, because the concepts of cause and effect express reciprocity, so must all substances express reciprocity. Reciprocity is thus a universal category and applies by necessity to whatever is.

Reciprocity is the negation of bad infinity in which we have a cause, the effect of which again is a cause of yet another effect and so on to infinity. In reciprocity, the effect 'bends back' into the cause of which it is an effect.[101] Bad infinity thus becomes true infinity.

Causality can no longer be regarded as being composed of two events. It cannot even be regarded as an event: In order to be classified as an event something must be temporally extended. Philosophical analysis has shown that causality is a concept, not a process.

As examples of reciprocity, Hegel mentions an organ in an organism.

---

101. "Although causality is not yet posited in its genuine determination, the progress, as an infinite progress from causes to effects, is truly sublated as progress in reciprocal action, because the rectilinear progression from causes to effects and from effects to causes is *curved* and *bent back* upon itself" (*Enz.* §154 Remark).

The condition of an organ influences the rest of the organism, just as the state of the organism as a whole influences each of its various organs. To take another example, one may ask whether the character and manners of a nation are the causes of its constitution and its laws, or if the manners and character are the effects. According to the category of reciprocity each is both a cause and an effect (*Enz.* §154 Remark).

In sum, reciprocity implies that everything is related to everything else by necessity. The category of reciprocity is the last category under the concept of essence, which implies that all previous categories—after having been logically cleansed—are sublated in that category. Whatever is, is tied together with everything else. Hence everything happens with necessity.

Necessity, however, differs from being forced. The necessity implied by the category of reciprocity is not imposed by force. This follows from what Hegel calls the "absolute idea." Whatever happens according to the absolute idea is not imposed by force, but in accord with each thing's own logical structure. It is therefore an expression of freedom, not of force. A necessity that is understood to be a necessity of the system with which something (or someone) is identical is precisely what counts as freedom: self-determination, as contrasted to external determination.[102]

Summary

Hegel grants that the section on essence is the most difficult in the *Logic*. A summary may thus be useful.

Essence is the truth of being. This is to say that, through the categories of essence, one gains a deeper understanding of being, an understanding acquired through the categories of reflection. The term 'reflection' is derived from the simple phenomenon of the reflection of a beam of light being reflected in a mirror back to its source.

Negation is the key to the categories of essence, just as it was to the categories of being. However, one difference between them is this: In the case of being, another concept establishes the negation by which identity is established; in the case of essence, negation is built into the concept itself. This is to say, no concept by itself possesses identity absolutely; no concept can do so because its negation is built into it. Hegel's reasoning is simply

---

102. "Generally speaking, the highest independence of man is to know himself as totally determined by the absolute Idea; this is the consciousness and attitude that Spinoza calls *amor intellectualis Dei*" (*Enz.* §158 Addition).

this: Absolute, abstract, or empty identity differs from concrete identity. "A planet is a planet," "a plant is a plant," and "magnesium is magnesium" exemplify abstract, empty identity. Such examples make it obvious that language idles in assertions of abstract empty identities, or, as Hegel puts it in this context, such statements make nonsense! Concrete identity, identity that contains negation, specifies both what something is and what it is not.

In relation to essence (the truth of essence), pure being, the being the truth of which is not yet grasped, is an appearance. Essence thus is identity that contains both pure being and true (sublated) being. It contains the essential as well as the inessential (that is, the negation of the essential). It is a unity of positivity and negativity.

This feature, that all categories of essence have their own negations built-in, that they are unities of positivity and negativity, is the key to all categories of essence. Consequently, every existing thing is a unity of identity and difference. Each existing thing in part relates to itself and is therefore a reflection-into-self; in part, each relates to something else and is therefore a reflection-into-other. Every existing thing therefore possesses both self-identity and the negation of this identity; its identity depends on something else.

That existence is a unity of self-identity, and the negation of this identity informs Hegel's special treatment of the formal logical principles of excluded middle and of contradiction. This is also the key to understanding Hegel's fundamental anti-Kantian metaphysical thesis about the identity of essence and the phenomenally given—of essence and appearance.

The relation of substance and accident is, by this reasoning, an identity; that is, both are active as well as passive. Accidents therefore react back onto substance. The result is reciprocity. That everything reciprocates with everything else means that everything forms a system, indeed, a system that has its ground in itself and therefore does not depend on anything else and is self-determined. This system unites necessity and freedom.

The Concept

Hegel's *Logic* is divided into two volumes. The first volume is called "The Objective Logic." Hegel calls it objective because it concerns the categories that necessarily apply to objects. This first volume has two books. The first book treats the categories of being, whereas the second book treats the categories of essence—the so-called categories of reflection.

The second volume Hegel calls "The Subjective Logic" or "The Doctrine of the Concept." The subjective logic is divided into two sections that, a bit confusingly, he names "subjectivity" and "objectivity," respectively. The first of these sections is a philosophical analysis of the concept as such, of judgment, and of syllogisms; the second is a philosophical analysis of mechanism, of chemism, and of teleology.

Subjectivity (The Concept as Such)

Hegel's discussion of "the concept" concerns the very concept of the concept. Two questions are central to his discussion: One concerns the dialectical development leading to the concept, the other concerns what could be called the validity of the concept.

Concerning the first question, the question about the dialectical path leading to the concept, what Hegel calls the genesis of the concept, we have seen how we were led from substance to causality and finally to reciprocity.[103] Recall that the category of reciprocity eliminates itself as a process

---

103. "Thus the dialectical movement of substance through causality and reciprocity is the immediate genesis of the concept" (*SL* 577). I translate here, as elsewhere, Hegel's '*Begriff*' as 'concept'; I see no sufficient reason to translate it as Miller does, as 'notion'.

and thus is transformed from one logical type to another: From being a process, it is transformed into a concept, a concept that implies that everything reciprocates with everything else. This in turn implies an all-comprehensive system in which everything occurs by necessity. Reciprocity is thus identical with the concept, or rather, the concept of the concept. The structure or "determinations" of the concept of reciprocity are necessary, and this necessity is self-determined. The concept of reciprocity is thus an expression of freedom.[104]

The concept of freedom is the key to understanding the nature of the concept of the concept. Obviously, freedom has meaning only if there is a subject—an I—which can exercise freedom. Hegel does not use exactly this kind of language. What he writes is this: "The concept when it has developed into a concrete existence that is itself free, is none other than the 'I' or pure self-consciousness" (*SL* 583).

The way Hegel conceives of the concept of the concept, as a subject or an 'I', is closely connected with Kant's transcendental apperception, which constitutes the condition for his "I think" or self-sonsciousness.[105] Because transcendental apperception is a universal concept—it is the logical condition for both consciousness and knowledge, hence it cannot itself be an object of consciousness, and must of course be universally valid—it follows that the 'I' likewise is a universal concept; to regard it as a psychological concept would be to commit a logical error. Nevertheless, Hegel emphasizes that the word 'I', because of the negativity built into it, is used to distinguish the user of the word from all others; each speaker excludes himself from them and opposes himself to them.[106]

Recall Hegel's famous claim from the *Phenomenology*, that ". . . everything turns on grasping and expressing the true not only as substance but equally as subject" (*PS* 9–10). What we now have arrived at is this: From

---

104. Cf. *Enz.* §158 Addition (quoted earlier, note 102) concerning the connection between necessity and freedom.

105. In the *Logic*, pretty much accepting Kant's identification of the I with transcendental apperception, Hegel writes: "It is one of the profoundest and truest insights to be found in the *Critique of Pure Reason* that the unity which constitutes the nature of the concept is recognized as the original synthetic unity of apperception, as unity of the *I think*, or of self-consciousness" (*SL* 584). Concerning the relation between Kant's transcendental apperception and Hegel's concept, see also Werner Marx *Hegel's Phenomenology of Spirit* (*op. cit.*), xix ff.

106. "The I as self-related negativity is no less immediately individuality or is absolutely determined opposing itself to all that is other and excluding it" (*SL* 583).

the concept of substance to reciprocity, and from there to necessity, which implies freedom, which in turn implies the I, we have the insight that substance is seen as identical with the subject.

Hegel criticizes the common view of what a concept is. The common view regards concepts abstractly. One gets such concepts by abstracting from empirical content. One gets such a concept (e.g., the concept of 'human being') by abstracting from the differences among all the beings classified as human beings. The more properties that are abstracted, the less content is left and the more instances it applies to. The concept 'European' applies to more instances than does, for example, the concept 'Dane'. To be a European requires fulfilling fewer criteria than does being a Dane. In addition to the criteria for being European, one must also satisfy the criteria for being a Dane. One may ask a European from which country she or he comes; but it would be a logical error to ask, for example, a Dane from which country she or he comes!

Hegel has a quite different view of the concept. According to Hegel, the concept is not abstract; it is concrete, or as he also says, it is a concrete universal. Nothing has been abstracted from the concrete concept or universal. On the contrary, all previous categories are accumulated (sublated) into it. The last category of essence is the category of reciprocity; in this category, the process or event was shown to be, not a process or an event, but rather a concept. This does not, however, entail that causality, just because it is neither a process nor two events nor even one event, does not exist. It means that causality has been logically cleansed and thus sublated in the concept. All the previous categories of being and essence were sublated and accumulated in reciprocity. Thus the concrete concept or concrete universal does not lack content; it is, on the contrary, enriched with the previous categories.[107]

Hegel's concept (of concept) contains what he calls three moments: universality, particularity, and individuality (*SL* 600). These three moments do not exist as three mutually independent entities or units. Rather, in order for a concept to make sense, that is, to fit in with or to accord with the logical grammar of language, it must be the case that these moments are built into, are interwoven with or, better, are inseparably integrated

---

107. ". . . the Concept . . . contains all the earlier determinations of thinking sublated within itself. . . . All the same, as we have said already, the Concept is also what is utterly concrete, precisely because it contains Being and Essence, and hence all the riches of both these spheres, within itself in ideal unity" (*Enz.* §160 Addition).

within the meaning of the concept. They can be distinguished only by philosophical analysis.

Note, first, that a grasp of universals is a necessary condition for being conscious of anything. As mentioned earlier, already in the *Phenomenology*, Hegel showed that even sense-certainty must conceive and identify its object by using universals. Not only 'here', 'now', and 'I' were shown to be universals, but, for example, the white color of an object is also a universal: The whiteness of the white color is a universal.[108] The universal does not, however, have an independent existence. Hegel is in this respect not a Platonist, but rather an Aristotelian.

If some animal is identified as an animal, what we observe is the particular animal; we identify it as a lion, a dog, a horse, or whatever. The universal animal as such we do not see; we do not see that which makes the animal an animal. Nevertheless, if that universal were not characteristic of the particular animal it would be impossible to say that we were observing an animal.[109]

That which constitutes the universal, that is, that which Hegel calls the permanent inward nature, is the substance, which must be understood as the law governing the particular universal, for instance, the universal that constitutes the animality of any particular animal.

In other words, that which is particular is at the same time also universal, and the universal is the particular; they necessarily go together and are inseparable.

As we have seen, the nerve of Hegel's dialectic is the concept of negation and the negation of the negation. They are negations necessitated by the emptiness and the uselessness of the abstract concept of identity, as opposed to the concrete concept of identity. To negate universality is to get the concept of particularity. By a negation of the negation, we, so to speak,

---

108. See my *From Radical Empiricism to Absolute Idealism* (*op. cit.*), 109–116.

109. Hegel expresses this quite clearly: " 'Animal as such' cannot be pointed out; only a definite animal can ever be pointed at. 'The Animal' does not exist; on the contrary, this expression refers to the universal nature of single animals, and each existing animal is something that is much more concretely determinate, something particularized. But 'to be animal', the kind considered as universal, pertains to the determinate animal and constitutes its determinate essentiality. If we were to deprive a dog of its animality we could not say what it is. Things as such have a persisting, inner nature, and an external thereness [*Dasein*, existence]" (*Enz.* §24 Addition 1).

return to the universal. This implies that the particular has been enriched by the universal through the first negation (and thus no longer *per impossibility* can be regarded as bare or pure particular) and is therefore an individual.[110]

It must be clearly understood that we are not here involved in a dialectical movement or process but in a dialectical analysis. Obviously, it is not the case that first we have the universal, then we get the particular, and finally get the individual. As we have seen, to have one of these moments is to have the other two as well. None of the three moments can have any meaning unless it is understood that all three moments by conceptual necessity are logically inseparable.

But even though they are inseparable—inseparable in the sense that they cannot exist independently of each other—they are nevertheless three distinct concepts. None of the three moments or concepts have the same connotation; because they have different connotations, they have different roles to play. We may draw a parallel to the category of reciprocity according to which there was no ontological difference between the cause and the effect. Together they did not constitute two events; instead they constituted a concept. Nevertheless, the concept of cause remains a distinct concept from the concept of effect. Likewise, the concept of universal is distinct from the concept of particularity, and both are distinct from the concept of individuality.

Judgment

The concept is the logical father of the judgment; or, rather, the judgment is built into the concept; it is in a sense the very essence of the concept. The judgment is a differentiation (Hegel's term is diremption) of the inseparable unity of the concept.[111] This diremption is the first, original, and decisive step (though here, too, the words 'first', 'original', and 'step' must not be conceived as events in time) that marks the logical transition from the concept to the judgment. Hegel emphasizes this logical founda-

---

110. "The object therefore has its objectivity in the concept and this is the unity of self-consciousness into which it has been received; consequently its objectivity, or the concept, is itself none other than the nature of self-consciousness, has no other moments or determinations than the I itself" (*SL* 585).

111. "Now consideration of the judgment can begin from the original unity of the concept, or from the self-subsistence of the extremes. The judgment is the self-diremption of the concept" (*SL* 625).

tion of the judgment by pointing to the etymological meaning of the German term for judgment, '*Urteil*': The original division.[112]

However, if a judgment is logical and results from the diremption of a concept, a contradiction seems inescapable: The three moments are logically inseparable, and yet the judgment that is logically built into the concept is precisely a self-diremption of the concept. This is a contradiction only if we fail to understand that they are inseparable insofar as, and only insofar as, regards independent existence—which, as we have seen, they cannot have. But they are obviously not inseparable insofar as the three moments or concepts have distinct connotations. (In modern terms, there is only a distinction of reason, but no real distinction, among them.)

A judgment, then, is constituted by the distinct connotations of the three moments or (partial) concepts; or, rather, it is constituted by the relation among them. This relation is expressed by the copula 'is'. The abstract formula of the judgment, the formula that becomes a judgment when it gets a content, is: "The individual is the universal."[113] The individual is the subject, and the universal the predicate. Recall that the individual is an individual only because the universal constitutes its essence. The universal is the soul or the substance of the individual, where the substance is defined by the law governing the universal or the concept. The predicate, Hegel stresses, is a predicate *of* the subject; it is a determination of the subject.[114]

According to Hegel, propositions and judgments differ. Although the proposition has the grammatical form of a judgment (it has a subject and a predicate), that does not suffice for being a judgment. In order to be a judgment, the predicate relates to the subject as a universal to a particular or individual. As an example of a proposition that does not qualify as a judgment, Hegel offers: "Aristotle died at the age of 73, in the fourth year of the 115th Olympiad" (*SL* 625). However, this proposition would be a judgment if there were some doubt about, for instance, his age at the time of his death and the proposition was asserted, then, on the strength of some reason, which could be classified as something universal (*SL* 625).

112. "It is thus the original division [*Teilung*] of what is originally one; thus the word *Urteil* refers to what judgment is in and for itself" (*SL* 625).

113. "The abstract judgment is the proposition: 'The singular is the universal'" (*Enz.* §166 Remark).

114. "[T]he copula 'is' attributes the predicate to the subject, that external, subjective *subsumption* is again sublated, and the judgment taken as a determination of the object itself" (*Enz.* §166 Remark).

Another example is this: "The news that my friend N. has died" is, Hegel says, a proposition (*SL* 626). The condition for being classified as a judgment is that there is a question whether he was really dead or only in a coma. Hegel appears to employ two criteria for a sentence to be a judgment. One criterion is that a sentence is a subject–predicate sentence; that is, that it falls under the formula: The individual is the universal, where the predicate is not related to the subject in an external way but explicates the universal built into the subject. The second criterion is that the sentence is used to eliminate possible doubt or to underline or establish that which the sentence says is, in fact, the case. In a way, Hegel here draws on the sense of judgment according to which a judgment is that which a judge pronounces; it is a verdict. It must be admitted that Hegel is by no means clear regarding this second criterion, and his commentators reflect this lack of clarity. It may be that Hegel is vaguely aware of the now common distinction between a sentence and its use. One and the same sentence may be used as an imperative or a permission, as a warning, or as an assertion. For example, if one wants to cross the street there may be a signal showing 'Wait' (an imperative), or there may be a signal showing 'Walk' (a permission). If Hegel indeed makes this distinction, it would be correct that the grammatical form of a sentence does not determine whether the sentence expresses a proposition or a judgment. In the *Encyclopaedia,* Hegel asserts that it would be absurd to say that the sentence "I slept well last night" could be turned into a judgment. Presumably the reason is that the predicate is not a universal and has only an external relation to the subject. It would be equally absurd to maintain that the sentence "Present arms!" could be turned into a judgment (*Enz.* §167 Remark). It has neither a subject nor a predicate and can never be rewritten in such a way that it fits into the formula: "The individual is the universal."

Sometimes Hegel talks about the copula as if it functioned to assert an identity between the subject and the predicate. Sometimes, however, the copula is meant to state that the predicate, although an essential part of the subject, nevertheless is not identical with it. And sometimes Hegel fails to distinguish between the 'is of predication' and the 'is of class membership'. To list, as he does, the two sentences (1) "the rose is red" and (2) "gold is a metal" as both being subject-predicate propositions (and judgments) is clearly mistaken. If instead of taking the two sentences "the rose is red" and "gold is a metal," we take the two sentences "the rose is red" and "red is a color" and regard both sentences as subject-predicate sentences, we should be able to infer that the rose is a color—an absurdity that reveals that we have committed a logical error, the error namely of failing to see that the sentence "red is a color" is not a subject-predicate sentence, but a sentence stating that the color red is a member of the class of colors.

It should be noted, in passing, following Bertrand Russell, that in sentences where the concept of existence is used as the grammatical predicate, the grammatical subject is not a logical subject, and that such sentences are not subject-predicate sentences at all.

The important thing to note, however, is that the judgment is logically derived from the concept of the concept, and that the concept is the result of the category of reciprocity, that is, from the last of the categories of essence—the category incorporating all the previous categories, and the category that marks the transition from event (e.g., causality) to the concept. It follows, as Hegel says, that "every thing is a judgment" (*Enz.* §167). It follows as well from what he says in the *Logic*: "The subject without predicate is what the thing without qualities, the thing in itself is in the sphere of appearance—an empty, indeterminate ground" (*SL* 628).

I shall not analyze or describe in detail Hegel's classifications of the different kinds of judgments (the qualitative judgment, the reflexive judgment, the necessary judgment, and the judgment of the concept). Only a few remarks will be made about these types of judgment—especially where they go beyond and diverge from the familiar.

Within the qualitative judgment, Hegel distinguishes between the positive (affirmative) judgment, the negative judgment, and the infinite judgment. In the *Encyclopaedia,* he mentions as instances of the infinite judgment "the mind is no elephant" and "a lion is no table" (*Enz.* §173). Curiously enough, Hegel says that such judgments are correct but absurd. In the *Logic*, where he mentions instances such as "spirit is not red," "the rose is not an elephant," and "the understanding is not a table," he says that these judgments are correct or true, but nonsensical and absurd (*SL* 642). It is difficult to agree with him when he says that what is absurd and nonsensical could have a truth-value. It seems to be without sense to try to verify that a spirit is not colored. What Hegel overlooks here is that the sentence "spirit is not red" is true (and therefore neither absurd nor nonsensical) if it is translated into a formal mode of speech: "The word 'spirit' is not a color-word."

Propositions like "the rose is not an elephant" or "spirit is not red" Hegel compares with identity propositions like "a lion is a lion" and "mind is mind." Such propositions are, he says, undoubtedly true, although they are not judgments at all (*Enz.* §173 Remark). Recall, however, that Hegel also says that such judgments are, and deserve to be, reputedly silly (cf. *Enz.* §115). This shows that Hegel faces grave difficulties reconciling the concepts of truth and absurdity with propositions that, from a logical point of view, are called silly. They do not even deserve to be called propositions—only pseudo-propositions.[115] In this connection Hegel also says: "The negatively infinite judgment, in which the subject has no relation whatever to the predicate, gets its place in formal logic solely as a nonsensical curiosity" (*Enz.* §173 Addition). Note the word 'nonsensical'.

Hegel's example of an objective instance of a negative infinite judgment is more interesting. A person who commits a crime such as theft demonstrates through his act that he has a different relation to the right of property than does the person who sues another party about the right to a definite piece of property. The person who commits a theft shows that he denies the right of the property-holder in general. But the person who sues another person demonstrates that he acknowledges the law in general; he contests only the other person's right to that particular piece of property. Through the civil-law suit he seeks a verdict concerning a particular instance of the law (*Enz.* §173 Addition).

Hegel's analysis of these examples of infinite judgments needs, however, a further explication and, it seems, correction. If a criminal commits theft, it follows from the concept of theft that a theft presupposes the right of property. If there were no such right it would be logically impossible to be a thief. The thief, in order to be a thief, must therefore know that there is such a right (if he is ignorant about it, he may be a backward person and may therefore not be responsible for his actions), and he consequently knows that he is a criminal. If this is so he cannot be said, as Hegel does, to deny or to reject the right of property; to reject it would be to reject that the concept of property could ever apply. The criminal does not deny the right of property; he disregards it. He disregards that which he quite well knows it is wrong to disregard. But whether we accept this correction to his analysis or not, the difference between the instances brought before the criminal courts and the cases brought before the civil courts still reveals a logical difference in the attitude toward the right of property—the difference between disregarding and disputing another person's right.

---

115. In the *Science of Logic*, he dismisses the sentence "God is god" as mere verbiage. He furthermore says that "nothing will be held to be more boring and tedious than conversation which merely reiterates the same thing, or than such talk which yet is supposed to be truth" (*SL* 415).

The *reflexive* judgment differs from the qualitative judgment. One way to explain this difference is to see the difference between the predicates appropriate to the two kinds of judgments. Examples of predicates belonging to the reflexive judgment include such predicates as perishable, useful, harmful, and hardness. Compare those predicates with predicates belonging to the qualitative judgment. Take for example the judgment 'the rose is red'. The difference between saying of something that it is red and saying that it is, for example, harmful is, among other things, that the existence of the predicate 'red' can be immediately verified by any person with normal color vision, whereas this is not the case with the predicates of reflexive judgments. They are about the relations the subject has to other objects or persons. Or in other words, predicates of reflective judgments say something about the laws that apply to the subjects of those judgments; they therefore express essential determinations (*SL* 643). One of Hegel's examples is the judgment "this plant is medicinal," which means that, because of the laws that govern the plant (and the human organism), it will have a positive effect on health (*Enz.* §175 Addition).

Within judgments of reflection, we must distinguish among singular judgments, particular judgments, and universal judgments. The singular judgment, however, turns out to entail the particular judgment. To say that this plant is medicinal or wholesome is not to restrict the predicate 'medicinal' or 'wholesome' to this individual plant. The expression 'this plant' cannot mean that this particular individual plant is the only plant in the world that is medicinal or wholesome. The singular judgment therefore changes into the judgment "Some plants are wholesome." It is interesting to note that, from the particular judgment, Hegel infers the negative judgment: "Some plants are not wholesome." This is contrary to the traditional square of opposition, which does not permit one to deduce a particular negative (O) judgment from a particular affirmative (I) judgment.[116] If I maintain that some plants are wholesome, the reason that I use the word 'some', and not 'all', may be that I am ignorant about whether all plants in fact are wholesome. In such a case, I have no justification whatever for maintaining the corresponding O-judgment: "Some plants are not wholesome." But if the reason is that I know that not all plants are wholesome, the best way to express that knowledge would be to say: "Some, but not all, plants are wholesome." If, however, I happen to know that all plants

116. On the traditional square of opposition, see Kneale and Kneale, *The Development of Logic* (Oxford: Clarendon Press, 1962), 55–56.

are wholesome, it surely would violate our language to use the statement: "Some plants are wholesome." The use of this expression in such a situation implies that some are but also that some are not. If a witness in court uses the term 'some', it must be clarified whether this is because he is ignorant or because he knows that only 'some' are not; if he knows that not only 'some' but 'all' are pertinent and he nevertheless uses the word 'some', he may be accused of lying—if not of perjury![117]

If I say about a plant that it is wholesome, I imply that there are (some) plants that are wholesome. But I also mean that all plants of this particular kind (e.g., camomile) are wholesome, whence I am justified in passing the universal judgment "All camomile-plants are wholesome" even though at the same time I can say only "Some plants are wholesome."

There is a difference, Hegel claims, between two kinds of universal judgments. One kind is the judgment that justifies its use of the word 'all' by the fact that no exceptions have so far been observed. This 'all' is rooted in enumeration. As an example of this, Hegel mentions the fact that all human beings in contrast to lower animals have ear lobes. This observation thus justifies the judgment: "All human beings possess ear lobes." If a person should be observed without ear lobes we should not therefore say that she or he was not a human being, that is, a being possessing the usual human characteristics and capacities. The other kind of universal judgment is justified not through enumeration and not by the fact that no exceptions have been discovered. It is justified by the fact that it belongs to the essence of the subject. Surely it does not belong to the essence of being a human being to possess ear lobes! It belongs to the essence of being a human to be able to exercise reason, that is, to act rationally, to be able to know the difference between good and evil, etc. As Hegel says, "it would not make sense to assume that Caius might perhaps be brave, learned, etc., and yet not be a man" (*Enz.* §175 Addition).

When we reach the point where we recognize that the predicate follows from the essence of the subject, we have a judgment of necessity. Such a judgment is not based on enumeration (like the judgment that all human beings have ear lobes). To negate the predicate would contradict the subject; this judgment is based on the essence of the subject. We express the

117. Cf. P. F. Strawson *Introduction to Logical Theory* (Oxford: Methuen & Co Ltd., 1952), 63ff. Concerning 'contextual implication', see P. H. Nowell-Smith *Ethics* (Harmondsworth: Penguin, 1954), 80ff.

change from the one kind of universal judgment to the other by using expressions such as *the* man or *the* plant.[118]

The Judgment of the Concept

Hegel divides judgments of the concept into assertoric judgments,
problematic judgments, and apodictic judgments. The best way to explain
the nature of these judgments is to begin with an example. If I assert that
"this house is a good house," I have simply asserted something about the
house, that it is more or less as it should be. To put it differently, I have
asserted that this particular house is as it should be according to the concept of a house; it meets the standards of being a house.[119]

In the assertoric judgment, an alleged fact is simply stated. However,
if a justification for the assertion is requested, then some reason(s) must be
given. If no reason whatever can be given, the judgment eliminates itself as
a judgment; nothing has in fact been asserted. If a reason is given, it ceases
to be an assertoric judgment and becomes either a problematic or an apodictic judgment. If I say "this house is good" but cannot give any reason
why I think it counts as a good house, I have asserted nothing. If the reasons I give provide some plausibility for the truth of the judgment—without, however, excluding reasons for either modifying or even denying my
judgment—the judgment is a problematic judgment. In this case, it is possible that the house is good, but it is also possible that it is not. If the reason
given for the judgment that the house is good is that all the standards prescribed for being a good house are satisfied and no arguments against the
judgment that it is a good house can be given, then the judgment is thus not
a problematic judgment but an apodictic judgment. A judgment is apodictic if the reasons for its truth suffice to make it absurd to say that one is
uncertain or that it is possibly true but not necessarily so.

---

118. "The advance from the allness-type of the judgment of reflection to the judgment of necessity can already be found in our ordinary consciousness when we say
that what pertains to all pertains to the kind and is therefore necessary. When we
say 'all plants', 'all men', etc., this is the same as if we had said 'the plant *as such*',
'man *as such*', etc." (*Enz.* §176 Addition).

119. "In this judgment, the concept is laid down as the basis, and since it is in relation to the object, it is an ought-to-be to which the reality may or may not be ade-
quate. Therefore it is only a judgment of this kind that contains a true appreciation;
the predicates good, bad, true, beautiful, correct, etc., express that the thing is
measured against its universal concept as the simply presupposed ought-to-be and
is, or is not, in agreement with it" (*SL* 657).

Because we say that a problematic judgment is only possible, whereas an apodictic judgment cannot be false, Hegel also calls these judgments of modality.

The Syllogism

To recall, the concept has three aspects or moments: the universal, the particular, and the individual. These aspects or moments are inseparable, that is, they do not exist as separate elements; what is universal is also particular, what is particular is also individual. They are ontologically identical; they have the same denotation. But although they have the same denotation, they do not have the same connotations. These differences in connotation are reflected in the logical structure of the judgment, namely, "The individual is the universal." The judgment results from analyzing the logical structure of the concept. The judgment is the logical unfolding of the connotations of the three distinct but inseparable elements of the concept.

This unfolding or analysis reveals, once again, three elements or concepts. However, the judgment, formally schematized as S—P, contains only two concepts: the subject and the predicate. The third concept makes the syllogism possible. This third element, usually called the middle term, is the particular, the common element or concept of two premises. The syllogism can then be schematized thus:

S—M
M—P
S—P

The middle term M is the particular. The function of the particular is to link together the two concepts, S and P, that is, link together the subject and the predicate—to link the individual to the universal in a logical relation.

To use Hegel's examples:

All men are mortal.
Gaius is a man.
Gaius is mortal.

In Hegel's terminology the term 'man' is the particular, the term 'mortal' is the universal, and the name 'Gaius' is the individual. Recall that, according to the concept, whatever is particular is also universal, and whatever is universal is also individual. The name Gaius, for instance, is a name of a person who is a universal because he is constituted by the universal 'human being'. But the universal 'human being' is a particular in relation to the concept 'mortal'. Every living being is mortal, but there are other living beings besides human beings.

As mentioned, the logical function of the particular is to establish the logical relation between the subject and the predicate. The particular is able to do so because it never exists merely as a particular, because so far as denotation is concerned, whatever is particular is also universal and individual—these three moments are inseparable. Nevertheless, the connotations of the three moments are distinct and distinguishable.

In the concept there is identity of denotation among the three moments. Judgments, however, explicate these three moments as three different concepts with three different connotations (although identical in denotation). The syllogism is constituted by the identity of the moments as we have them in the concept, but it also deals with these three moments as three concepts with different connotations. By establishing this unity with the three identical moments in the concept, the syllogism thus establishes the identity of the concept and the judgment.[120]

One of Hegel's central claims is this: Everything is a syllogism (*Enz.* §181 Remark). This is important, and it follows necessarily from Hegel's logical system. We have seen that according to the category of reciprocity, the categories are accumulated in the category of the concept. A logical analysis of the concept of the concept leads by necessity to the judgment and from there to the syllogism. The principles determining the logical analysis are, to recall, (1) the principle of negation, including the negation of negation, and (2) the Spinozistic principle, to determine is to negate.[121] Because the real is the rational, it follows that reality is determined by, it is an expression of, the categories; thus reality is also determined by and is an expression of a syllogism.[122]

Hegel divides syllogisms according to the division of judgments.

---

120. Hegel writes: "The syllogism is the unity of the concept and the judgment; it is the concept as the simple identity into which the form-distinctions of the judgment have returned . . ." (*Enz.* §181).

121. "*Omnis determinatio est negatio*" (*Enz.* §91 Addition).

122. "[N]ot only is the syllogism rational, but everything rational is a syllogism" (*SL* 664).

Thus he presents a syllogism of existence, a syllogism of reflection, and a syllogism of necessity. Because the foundation of the concept, the judgment, and the syllogism is constituted by the three concepts of the universal, the particular, and the individual, Hegel does not schematize the various syllogisms in the traditional way.[123] Instead of schematizing a syllogism of the first figure as

S—M
M—P
S—P

Hegel uses the letter I for individuals, P for particulars, and U for universals, and instead of writing in the preceding form, he simply writes it as: I—P—U.

The disjunctive syllogism, as one of the syllogisms of necessity, has a special position. As an example of a disjunctive judgment, Hegel takes the following: "A work of poetic art is either epic or lyric or dramatic." What characterizes such a judgment is that the genus (here, 'A work of poetic art') is the sum of the species (that is, epic or lyric or dramatic poetry), and vice versa, the sum of the species is the genus. The disjunctive syllogism is consequently either:

A work of poetic art is either epic or lyric or dramatic.
This work of poetic art is epic.
It is therefore neither lyric nor dramatic.

Or

A work of poetic art is either epic or lyric or dramatic.
This work of poetry is neither epic nor lyric.
It is therefore dramatic.

In the disjunctive syllogism, the particular changes its logical character. In the preceding example, we have the two concepts: 'all poetic works' and 'this poetic work'. The particular—the concept that changes its logical

---

123. On the traditional syllogistic figures, see Kneale and Kneale, *The Development of Logic* (*op. cit.*), 68–81.

character—mentions all possible cases of poetic works. That is, the particular, whose function is to connect the individual and the universal, itself contains both of these. The disjunctive syllogism therefore does not conform to the typical scheme of a syllogism. Hegel expresses this by saying that, because of the complete specification of all possible species, the disjunctive syllogism changes from the mediated to the immediate.[124]

Obviously, the disjunctive syllogism (or alleged syllogism) presupposes that we are able to enumerate all the possible species of a genus, that is, all the species that exhaust the genus. If we cannot do this, we cannot validly infer the species of the individual. This syllogism also presupposes that the disjunction is exclusive, that it is not a disjunction which says: Either A or B or maybe both, but at least one of them.

In general, we can express the disjunctive syllogism thus:

> A is either B or C or D.
> But A is B.
> Therefore, A is neither C nor D.

Or:

> A is either B or C or D.
> But A is neither C nor D.
> Therefore, A is B. (*SL* 701–02).

Notice that B or C or D are the names of the objects (the species) that determine the universal—the genus—A. B, C, and D, so to speak, exhaust the universal. They unpack all the possible species of the genus.

The difference between this form and syllogisms with a particular serving as a middle term is clearly seen if we compare the preceding syllogism with, for example, this syllogism:

---

124. "The syllogism is *mediation*, the complete concept in its *positedness*. Its movement is the sublating of this mediation, in which nothing is in and for itself, but each is only by means of an other. The result is therefore an *immediacy* which has issued from *sublating the mediation*, [it is] a *being* which is just as identical with the mediation and with the concept that has produced itself from and in its otherness. This *being* is therefore a *thing* [*eine Sache*] that is in and for itself—objectively" (*SL* 704; tr. revised.—ed.).

All men are mortal.

Gaius is a man.

Therefore, Gaius is mortal.

Here the concept of man serves as a middle term and therefore does not figure in the conclusion. It is important to notice that 'man' is a concept or universal under which Gaius (the subject) is subsumed. In other words, when A is not subsumed under B, C, and D, but is identical with B, C, and D, then the subject in the syllogism is subsumed under the middle term. Of course, Gaius is not identical with all the infinitely many species of humanity! In this syllogism, the conclusion that Gaius is mortal is an inference; it is mediated. In the disjunctive semisyllogism, that A is neither C nor D, or that A is B, is not inferred but is immediate. The object is thus seen to be a direct consequence of, or rather to be built into, the concept.

The Object

As we have just seen, the mediated disjunctive syllogism turns out to be immediate objectivity. The disjunctive syllogism thus marks the transition from concept to objectivity.[125] But a transition does not mean a break. The concept of an object is not to be understood as something outside the logical system; on the contrary, it presupposes it: Without the logic of the concept, there could not be a concept of the object.

By reaching this conclusion Hegel has reached the view that he regards as the basic metaphysical truth. From Kant through Fichte and Schelling, the problem of the relation between subject and object or substance has been central. Despite Kant's ingenuity, his transcendental philosophy led to an impasse: The concept of the thing in itself was unacceptable and required a conceptual rectification. Fichte was the first to attempt this rectification. Fichte distinguished between the finite I (the individual human being) and the infinite I. The infinite I constituted the ground for finite minds and empirical objects. Schelling began his philosophical career as a Fichtean, but later broke with him. Instead of the infinite I, Schelling based his philosophy on reason. Reason, according to Schelling, is the formal cause of whatever is. That is, reason is the formal cause not only of reason in individual minds but also of nature. Hegel's logic may be seen as laying out—mapping out—the logical structure of

---

125. "Finally, objectivity is the immediacy to which the concept determines itself by the sublation of its abstraction and mediation" (*SL* 708). Furthermore, "The object is, as we have seen, the syllogism, whose mediation has been sublated [*ausgeglichen*] and has therefore become an immediate identity" (*SL* 711).

reason. Hegel's *Logic* thus gives us the logical structure of categories that permeates nature as well as thought and also manifests itself in individual minds. Hegel's logic is thus an ontological logic. Whatever is, is determined by the categories.[126]

Hegel emphasized, like Schelling, that to speak of reason or thought as "the heart and soul of the world" (as Hegel puts it) is of course not to ascribe consciousness to nature. Hegel therefore recommends that we speak of nature as the system of unconscious thought. Schelling called nature the invisible spirit (*Geist*) or petrified intelligence—an expression Hegel adopts (*Enz.* §24 Addition). Recall, here again, Hegel's remark in the "Preface" to the *Phenomenology*: "In my view, which can be justified only by the exposition of the system itself, everything, turns on grasping and expressing the true not only as substance but equally as subject" (*PS* 9–10).

The concept of object is logically tied to the concept; as a logical descendant it has inherited its logical features. The object is consequently an object in which there is no distinction between substance and accidents, between the thing and its properties, between the whole and its parts, etc. All these distinctions are, however, sublated in the concept.[127] Hegel's philosophical analysis takes us step by step from the object as mechanical object to the object as chemical object to the ultimate and decisive step: the object as a teleological concept.

The Object as Mechanical Object

According to what Hegel calls the formal mechanism, the object results from the disjunctive syllogism in which mediation becomes immediate. In the object, there is no distinction between properties or accidents; hence the object as such can be determined only by what is outside it.[128] That is, only the impact made on it by other objects can have any effect on

---

126. "Thus *logic* coincides with *metaphysics*, with the science of *things* grasped in *thoughts* that used to be taken to express the *essentialities* of *things*" (*Enz.* §24).

127. Hegel uses the term '*untergegangen*' which partly means perished and partly means went down to the bottom—which in this context means down to the bottom of the concept, or in other words, it can be taken to have the same meaning as 'sublated'.

128. "This is what constitutes the character of *mechanism*, namely, that whatever relation obtains between the things combined, this relation is one *extraneous* to them that does not concern their nature at all" (*SL* 711).

it. This is a mechanical system reminiscent of Hobbes's "bodies in motion." Movement and pressure are the only forces capable of causing changes in the world. Hegel, however, rejects this model. Hobbes's atomic theory is not tied to a logical system; it is not the outcome of such a system, but rather its presupposition. In Hobbes's theory, mechanism is a premise; in Hegel's, the object is a conclusion of a syllogism. Furthermore, the atom is not an aggregate, whereas the Hegelian object, as a logical descendant of the concept, is analyzable into the moments of the universal, the particular, and the individual, and there is nothing that is not all three moments at once. Each object is consequently a plurality of objects. This plurality Hegel characterizes as an indeterminate determinateness.[129]

However, a purely formal mechanical model is not sufficient: There are phenomena that defy assimilation to it. Several kinds of organic processes and several phenomena classified as psychological are not explicable in terms of external mechanical forms; even within the physical sciences the model is insufficient (*Enz.* §195 Addition).

The Object as Chemical Object

Mechanism—the view that everything in the world of objects is explicable exclusively by appeal to forces outside the object, where each object is totally independent of all other objects—cannot be upheld; hence it is superceded by chemism. According to chemism two different objects are attracted to each other and become one object. That object integrates their differences. Those differences are neutralized; this is why Hegel calls this object a neutralized object. It is neutral because it is the end-product of the chemical process released by the tension (chemical potential) that started the process.[130]

When Hegel uses the term 'strive' (*streben*) to describe or to explain the attraction between two objects, the word should not be taken in the

---

129. "Because this indeterminate determinateness is essential to the object, the latter is within itself a plurality of this kind, and must therefore be regarded as a composite or aggregate. It does not, however, consist of atoms, for they are not objects because they are not totalities" (*SL* 712).

130. "The product is neutral, that is, a product in which the ingredients, which no longer can be called objects, have lost their tension and with it those properties which belonged to them as tensed" (*SL* 729).

usual psychological sense; the word is used to distinguish chemical from mechanical forces.

The Object as Teleological Object

The mechanical and the chemical models of the object imply a deterministic conception of the objective world—a world in which changes and processes are caused by external forces, not by the objects themselves. None of the objects, according to these models, are self-determined. Opposed to this is the teleological view, according to which the final determing cause is, not external, but an internal cause. Mechanical and chemical processes constitute necessary conditions for understanding and explaining mechanical or chemical processes, but they do not constitute sufficient causes. A sufficient cause requires explaining mechanical and chemical processes as leading to a certain end. Mechanical and chemical processes constitute efficient causes; the end, however, constitutes the final cause (*SL* 734).

Hegel praises Kant for his distinction between external and internal teleology—a distinction Hegel accepts. External teleology is philosophically untenable, whereas internal teleology is a category and therefore universally valid. The criterion for distinguishing these two kinds of teleology is this: According to external teleology, the end is distinct from the process leading to the end. For example, the process of building a house is distinct from the purpose of building it. The purpose is to make a place in which to live. In internal teleology, the processes leading to the end and the end itself are not distinct.

In the opening lines of his chapter on teleology, Hegel states that whenever a purpose is discerned an intelligence is assumed as author. Hegel warns against this assumption. Often it has its roots in a well-meant wish to display, in a naive way, the wisdom of god.[131]

---

131. "[S]ince in the teleological approach we also have to deal with the well-intentioned concern to demonstrate the wisdom of God, as it specifically announces itself in nature, it must be remarked that, in all this searching out of the purposes for which things serve as means, we do not get beyond the finite, and we can very easily end up in lame reflections; for example, when it is not only the vine that is considered under the aspect of the well-known utility that it has for men, but the cork tree, too, is considered in its relation to the stoppers cut from its bark in order to seal wine bottles. Whole books used to be written in this spirit, and it is easy to see that neither the true interest of religion nor that of science can be advanced this way" (*Enz.* §205 Addition).

In addition to the naiveté of external teleology, there are other more logical kinds of criticism of it. I cannot build a house without using certain materials. I may use lumber, but the tree from which I get the timber does not exist simply to provide materials for building houses. It may or it may not. In some cases lumber may be used to build houses; in other cases, it may be used to make furniture, or it may be used for fuel in fireplaces. In other words, it is quite arbitrary whether a particular tree will be used this way or that way, or will be put to any use at all. A tree is an element in a teleological process only if it happens to be used as a means for obtaining a certain end. If it is not used, it has no (external) teleological function.

External teleology, furthermore, is an expression of bad infinity; whatever is a means to something else has itself come into existence by something else whose existence in turn is due to something else, and so forth to infinity.

The criterion of internal teleology is, as mentioned, that there is no distinction between the end and the process leading to it. In order to understand Hegel's conception of internal teleology, recall Aristotle's conception of internal teleology. According to Aristotle, every substance is a special kind of thing: a certain kind of stone, a certain kind of animal, a certain kind of plant, or whatever. A thing or substance is what it is due to certain features or properties—features or properties that define the thing as being this specific thing or substance; they constitute what Aristotle calls the form of the thing. The process that takes place in, for example, a swan's egg that leads to a swan (rather than to a duck or any other kind of organism) is an example of internal teleology. It is a goal-directed process in which the process is one with the goal. The fully developed swan is the end of a continuous process.

The difference betwen external and internal teleology is clear: To build a house is to impose the form of a house on some materials—a form the materials do not possess by themselves. On the other hand, the form of a swan is already in the swan's egg; it does not have to be imposed upon it, it always possessed it. Whereas the process leading from means to ends in external teleology expresses bad infinity, no such infinity is involved in internal teleology. When the process has led from the swan's egg to the swan, the process is completed. Nature does not require that process to continue; the full-grown swan is the final end of the process.

Another important difference between external and internal teleology is that building a house, for example, is based on a decision, the decision to satisfy the wish to have a place to live. There is no such decision behind processes that express internal teleology. No one decides or determines the processes leading from the swan's egg to the swan. Those processes do not result from a prior decision based on knowledge of their nature. Internal teleological processes characterize the processes in all organisms. The functions of my organs—heart, kidneys, lungs, etc.—constitute necessary conditions for sustaining my life. Usually we explain the functions of these organs by explaining how they function and why such a function is a necessary condition; if the organs ceased to function, we would die. Kant, for instance, admitted as much. However, Kant denied that the purpose of preserving life could serve as an explanation; to explain a process by pointing to its purposeful result could not be justified. Instead Kant classified the purpose as a regulative (not a constitutive) idea. The purpose could help to set up a hypothesis; whether the hypothesis is correct can be verified only by an investigation of the relevant scientific processes (i.e., mechanical, chemical, and other verifiable processes).

We saw how reciprocity led us from event to concept. The concept possesses necessity—a necessity due to nothing but itself and therefore is self-determining. What is self-determined enjoys freedom—it is what freedom means. Reciprocity is therefore not only a logical transition from event to concept, but it is also a transition to subject. Or, rather, through reciprocity, we see that substance is identified with subject.[132]

Furthermore, we have seen that the concept implies objectivity; this concept takes us from mechanism and chemism (both of which turn out to be insufficient) to teleology. As a category, teleology (internal teleology) expresses a necessary feature of all reality or actuality. In contrast to external teleology, which runs to bad infinity, internal teleology expresses true infinity; it has within itself the means for its end. It is the self-related and self-determined concept. Because to be self-determined is to be determined by nothing outside itself, it follows that it is free. Whatever enjoys

---

132. "Hence the reciprocity is the appearance that again sublates itself, the revelation that the *show* of causality in which the cause appears *as* cause, *is show*. This infinite reflection-into-self, namely, that being is in and for itself only in so far as it is posited, is the *consummation of substance*. But this consummation is no longer *substance* itself but something higher, the *concept*, the *subject*. The transition of the relation of substantiality takes place through its own immanent necessity and is nothing more than the manifestation of itself, that the notion is its truth, and the freedom is the truth of necessity" (*SL* 579–80).

freedom is a subject. In other words: Objectivity implies teleology, which implies freedom, which therefore implies subjectivity. We are thus required to arrive at the central Hegelian thesis of the identity between substance and subject—between being and thought. The unity of substance and subject Hegel calls "idea."[133]

133. Before I begin the description of the idea, it may be useful to end this part of Hegel's logic—a part which has taken us by philosophical analysis from being to thought—by quoting some parts of his lengthy comments on §24 in the *Encyclopaedia*: " If we say that thought, *qua* objective, is the inwardness of the world, it may seem as if consciousness is being ascribed to natural things. But we feel a repugnance against conceiving the inner activity of things to be thinking, since we say that man is distinguished from what is merely natural by virtue of our thinking. In this view, we would have to talk about nature as a system of thought without consciousness, or an intelligence which, as Schelling says, is petrified. So in order to avoid misunderstanding, it is better to speak of 'thought-determinations' instead of using the expression 'thoughts'.

"In line with what has been said so far, then, the logical is to be sought in a system of thought-determinations in which the antithesis between subjective and objective (in its usual meaning) disappears. This meaning of thinking and of its determinations is more precisely expressed by the Ancients when they say that *nous* governs the world, or by our own saying that there is reason in the world, by which we mean that reason is the soul of the world, inhabits it, and is immanent in it, as its own, innermost nature, its universal" (*Enz.* §24 Addition).

The Idea

The Idea as Unity of Subjectivity and Objectivity

As just stated, the idea is the unity of subjectivity (the concept) and objectivity. The idea is the truth.[134]

It is important to understand that all the categories—both the categories of being and essence and the categories of the concept—by philosophical, dialectical necessity have not only led to the idea but also to the fact that they all are sublated in the idea. An example of such a category is the category of reciprocity. This category, as we saw, implies that cause and effect do not refer to two different events, not even to one event, but to a concept. According to this concept, the difference between the concept of a cause and the concept of an effect is sublated. But to be sublated is not to be eliminated. The sublated categories still exist in the sense that it still has meaning to speak (e.g., about the cause as an event that constitutes the explanation of the occurrence of another event): The fact that one billiard ball is rolling is explained by another fact, the fact, namely, that another billiard ball pushed it.

The idea is thus identical with all that is deduced in the *Logic* about the logical structure of being, essence, and the concept. All the categories are, so to speak, absorbed into the idea. The idea is thus the end of the conceptual movement, the end that results in identifying subjectivity and objectivity. I want to emphasize again that conceptual movement is only called movement figuratively. The idea does not result from a process; it has not become what it is as the end-product of a temporal process. That this is not the case follows already from the fact that Hegel identifies the

---

134. "The idea is what is true *in and for itself, the absolute unity of concept and objectivity*" (*Enz.* §213).

112

absolute idea with god, and it surely would be against a fundamental view of and meaning of the word 'god' that it should refer to a being who came into existence at a certain time. It does take time, however, for the individual to obtain a full understanding of god (of the absolute idea). Such an understanding results, according to Hegel, from the study and understanding of his *Logic*.[135]

As indicated, the idea as a universal and valid concept could be asserted on the basis of internal teleology—a teleology in which the goal-directed process and the goal the process is directed at are identical. This identity, as shown, implies the identity of subjectivity and objectivity; that is, it implies the idea.

The idea has three aspects: (1) life, (2) cognition, and (3) the absolute idea.

Life

The unity of soul and body, Hegel claims, is a consequence of the idea as a unity of subject and object.[136] Hegel further claims that the immediate idea is life and that the concept of life is the soul that is realized in the body (*Enz.* §216). In other words, when Hegel speaks of soul and body, he does not avow Cartesian dualism. The soul is identical with the body, with the organism; due to the soul the organism is an organism. A dead organism is therefore not an organism.[137] Hegel thus agrees with Aristotle: A severed hand is only nominally a hand (*Enz.* §216 Addition). A part of an organism

---

135. In the *Encyclopaedia* §210, Hegel uses the expression "the realized end." This expression seems to indicate that the end (the idea) is the result of a process. That this is not the case, however, can be seen from what he says in the Addition to §212: "The accomplishing of the infinite purpose consists . . . only in sublating the illusion that it has not yet been accomplished. . . . This is the illusion in which we live. . . ."

136. "The idea can be grasped as *reason* (this is the proper philosophical meaning of 'reason'); and further as the *subject-object*, as the *unity of the ideal and the real*, *of the finite and the infinite*, *of the soul and the body*, as the *possibility that has its actuality in itself*, as that whose *nature* can be *comprehended only* as *existing*, and so forth" (*Enz.* §214).

137. Crawford Elder expresses this very clearly: "The role of each organ is, in general terms, the same: each functions so as to maintain health and functioning in the organism as a whole; and hence each organ can be seen as motivated by a purpose of there being ongoing purposive activity as such. An organ contributes to ongoing organ operation by restoring or repairing some other organ," *Appropriating Hegel* (*op. cit.*), 36.

that is no longer part of it—is no longer part of its unity—becomes merely a mechanical–chemical object.

The concept of life has, like all Hegel's concepts, three moments: (1) the universal, (2) the particular, and (3) the individual. Life as a universal is sensibility. An organism is constantly exposed to sense-impressions. This plurality of sense-impressions, however, are all related by the living organism to its self-feeling.[138] Sense-impressions—the sensation of, for example, pain, itches, and heat—are all 'my' (someone's) sensations. The external plurality of sensations is thus in this way conceived through the unity of the organism, that is, through what expresses the universal.[139]

Life as particular is irritability. This is the organism's reaction to sense-impressions (sensibility). This is the reaction of the unity (the universal) to the plurality of sense-impressions. The fact that irritability is regarded as a reaction to sense-impressions may be seen as an instance of the category of reciprocity: reacting to a stimulus (e.g., I scratch in reaction to an itch; I withdraw my hand in reaction to the burning sensation received from a hot plate, etc.) is parallel to the cause-and-effect relation. We saw that there was no difference between the concept of the cause and the concept of the effect. Likewise, we may say that, insofar as the reaction to a sense-impression falls under the category of reciprocity, the difference between the reaction and the sense-impression to which one reacts vanishes.[140]

Life as the individual is also expressed, finally, through reproduction. This is a continuous process of renovation and regeneration. This process is necessary for the existence of an organism. It expresses the built-in self-preservation of an organism; it is an expression of individuality. One may

138. "The individual external determinateness, a so-called *impression*, returns from its external and manifold determination into this simplicity of *self-feeling*" (*SL* 768).

139. "Sensibility may therefore be regarded as the determinate being of the inwardly existent soul, since it receives all externality into itself, while reducing it to the perfect simplicity of self-identical universality" (*SL* 768; tr. revised.—ed.).

140. Two so very different philosophers—different with respect both to their metaphysical views and their place in the history of philosophy—as Hegel and Gilbert Ryle are almost holding hands on this particular point. In his essay "Feelings," Ryle asserts that the itch and the scratch are logically connected, connected in the same sense that the itch can be defined only in terms of the reaction, i.e., the scratch (*Collected Papers*; New York: Barnes & Noble, 1971; 2:278f). In the Danish language the verb to 'klø' may mean both the sense-impression and the reaction, that is, both to itch and to scratch.

say that it belongs to the essence of any organism to preserve itself. One of Spinoza's main metaphysical theses is that whatever has being attempts to preserve itself in being. One could put this negatively: It is contrary to the functioning of any organism that it should break down or destroy itself. This is no merely empirical truth. That it is not based on observation follows from the fact that, if it were not the case, there would be no organisms at all.

Hegel has often been criticized for this section on the concept of life. Hegel is clearly committed to the view that whatever is, is a syllogism—a syllogism that operates with the three concepts: the universal, the particular, and the individual. Although his arguments surely are not without force—the arguments that the life-concepts (of sensibility, irritability, and reproduction) express the universal, the particular, and the individual, respectively—they cannot but appear somewhat strained. The suspicion that, in order to fit the three life-concepts into his scheme, they are contorted to fit a Procrustean bed, is not easy to reject.[141]

The Life Process

The relation between an organism and inorganic nature—the other that, so to speak, envelops it—characterizes the life process. The inorganic is related to the organic either as something towards which the organic is indifferent or, more often, the organic either needs and consequently attempts to acquire, or the inorganic is something it fights against or attempts to negate.

The organism strives, it must strive, to incorporate whatever in inorganic nature is necessary for its survival; it strives to make it a part of itself. The inorganic that is assimilated into the organic is "virtually the same as what life is actually."[142] In other words, the organic and the inorganic are

141. For a discussion of the functionalist core of Hegel's account of teleology, see Willem deVries, "The Dialectic of Teleology" *Philosophical Topics* 19, No. 2, 1992, 51–70.

142. "The living being confronts an inorganic nature to which it relates as the power over it, and which it assimilates. The result of this process is not, as in the case of the chemical process, a neutral product in which the independence of the two sides that confronted one another is sublated; instead, the living being proves itself to be what overgrasps its other, which cannot resist its power. Inorganic nature, which is subdued by the living being, suffers this subjection because it is *in-itself* the same as what life is *for-itself*. So in the other the living being only comes together with itself. When the soul has fled from the body, the elementary powers of objectivity come into play. These powers are, so to speak, continually ready to pounce, to begin their process in the organic body, and life is a constant struggle against them" (*Enz.* §219 Addition).

both identical and different. They are identical insofar as both the organic and the inorganic fall under the idea; they are different because there is, after all, a difference between what is inorganic and what is organic.

As we have seen, Hegel's philosophical analysis leads to the idea, to the identity of subjectivity and objectivity. However, as we have also seen, the dialectical advance toward the idea is conditioned by the concept of sublation. Sublation does not imply that the sublated distinctions are eliminated; they are preserved; their conceptual existence is preserved in that into which they are sublated. Thus it is correct to say that, when the organic incorporates or assimilates the inorganic, the inorganic is united with the organic.[143] It also implies, however, that the organic—the living individual—insofar as it is destined constantly to strive to preserve itself, must be regarded as an imperfect being. The living individual must continually, so to speak, create itself. It never transcends its limitations.

The life of the idea is actualized in the innumerable living organisms, each of which strives to preserve the kind (*Gattung*) they represent and which they, through reproduction, strive to preserve forever. Individuals are born and they die. This process expresses bad infinity. The death of each individual person is necessitated, Hegel contends, by the logical fact that a living individual is a contradiction. It is a contradiction between the universal concept, the kind, and the living individual. This contradiction, according to Hegel, necessitates that all individuals must die.[144]

---

143. Hegel also applies the concepts of the organic and the inorganic in connection with education (*Bildung*): "In this respect formative education, regarded from the side of the individual, consists in his acquiring what thus lies at hand, devouring his inorganic nature, and taking possession of it for himself" (*PS* 16).

144. "The living being dies because it is the contradiction of being *in-itself* the universal, the genus, and yet existing immediately only as a singular being. In death the genus proves itself to be the power over the immediately singular being.—For the animal, the process of the genus is the highest point of its living career. But the animal does not succeed in being for-itself in its species; instead, it succumbs to the power of the latter. The immediate living being mediates itself with itself in the process of the genus; and in this way it elevates itself above its immediacy, but always just to sink back into it again. So, to start with, life simply runs its course into the spurious infinity of the infinite progress. But what, according to the concept, is brought about through the process of life is the sublation and overcoming of the immediacy in which as life the idea is still entangled" (*Enz.* §221 Addition).

The Idea as Cognition
The Theoretical Idea

Let me emphasize once again: The idea implies the identity of subject and object. If subject and object are identical, how are we to understand cognition? Cognition concerns the relation between subject and object. The subject strives to acquire knowledge of an object. For this to make sense, there must not be an identity between the subject and the object the subject attempts to know. In other words, a paradox seems inescapable: The object of knowledge is different from the subject, and yet it is not different. Nevertheless, anyone who has followed the dialectical development up to the idea will realize that this is only an apparent paradox, because the identity of subject and object involved in the idea is, as emphasized earlier, an identity of the universal subject, not the individual, empirical subject. It would indeed be absurd to assert that there should be identity between me and the mosquito I kill. It is not absurd, however, to assert that there is identity between the universal subject and the objective world—identity in the sense that the categories of the universal subject (the world of subjectivity) are identical with the categories of the objective world. The difference between Kant and Hegel is very important here. To Kant the categories of the understanding constitute necessary conditions of knowledge; at the same time those categories were regarded as a kind of tool applied to the object (the stuff) in order that the object could be an object of knowledge. Knowledge resulted from applying categories to the object (the stuff). What this object, this stuff, was in itself would forever be a secret—a puzzle. Or more correctly: The very assumption of the existence of a thing in itself verges on a meaningless assumption. Another related difference is that Kant's categories are abstract (and therefore empty), whereas Hegel's categories are concrete concepts.

The Idea as Volition—the Good
The Practical Idea

Hegel's analysis of volition and the good is, like so much of Hegel's thought, inspired by ancient Greek philosophy. The tyrant who does whatever he likes or wants to do is not, Plato teaches us, necessarily doing what he wills. Volition is not identical with one's wants, wishes, and desires. Wishes, wants, and desires are psychological concepts. It would be no contradiction to say that I want something that is evil. But according to

Platonic philosophy, volition is logically connected with the good. Therefore the tyrant who desires something that is evil is not desiring that which he wills. That which one wills is by necessity the good. Having to choose between two possibilities, one of which is better than the other, one chooses the better one. Why? Because it is part of what is meant by the word 'better'. To say about something that it is good is to say that it is more than average. To say that it is the best is to say that if there is no overriding reason not to choose it, it is the one to choose. If the tyrant chooses that which is bad, harmful, or even evil, it is because he is either ill-informed, ignorant, or does not know any better. In other words, to act according to will requires that one knows what the good is. And to know is to know the idea—the theoretical idea.

The difference between cognition, the theoretical idea, and volition, the practical idea, is that cognition takes "the world as it is," whereas the practical idea "takes steps to make the world what it ought to be."[145]

The world as it is, as it in fact necessarily must be, is a world in which subject and object (thought and being) are identical. Obviously, to say that the world is as it necessarily must be, is the same as to say that it is the world as it ought to be.[146]

The finite and philosphically enlightened consciousness experiences the world as a world of change, not as a world in which there is identity between subject and object. That is, it experiences a world in which neither the theoretical idea nor the practical idea is (fully) realized. But with growing philosophical understanding, it will be realized that even a Heraclitean world is a world in which, through all changes, subject and object are identical. This is therefore also a world in which not only the theoretical idea but also the practical idea constantly is displayed.[147]

---

145. "Whereas the task of intelligence is simply to take the world as it *is*, the will, in contrast, is concerned to make the world finally what it *ought* to be" (*Enz.* §234 Addition).

146. It should not be forgotten that when Hegel in the *Logic* analyzes such concepts as 'the good', 'will', and 'volition', it is a display of—an exercise in—philosophical analysis of these concepts. It is an essay about neither ethics nor psychology, but about the logical relations among these concepts.

147. "As a result the *truth* of the good is *posited*—as the unity of the theoretical and the practical idea: [the truth] that the good has been reached in and for itself—that the objective world is in this way in and for itself the idea positing itself eternally as *purpose* and at the same time bringing forth its actuality through [its] activity" (*Enz.* §235).

This could easily be misunderstood. It could be understood to mean that the good is constantly becoming. Such a misunderstanding is not made easier to avoid when Hegel writes: "the final purpose of the world, the good, only *is*, because it constantly brings itself about" (*Enz.* §234 Addition). It must be stressed, however, that the good is not constantly *created* but constantly *displayed*. The unity of theoretical and practical idea constitutes the absolute idea, and the absolute idea is, to recall, not the result of a process. It has never not been. As Hegel puts it: "the objective world is . . . in and for itself the Idea positing itself eternally as *purpose* and at the same time bringing forth its actuality through [its] activity" (*Enz.* §235).

A related misunderstanding assumes that anything that "is" is "actual," so that Hegel would thus endorse the rationality of anything that is. Hegel emphatically distinguishes what is "actual" from what is merely "real" or what merely "exists" or simply "is." Hegel's slogan does not have the conservative or reactionary implications so often imputed to his philosophy (*Enz.* §6 Remark).

The Absolute Idea

The absolute idea is the culmination of philosophical thinking. This thinking has led to an understanding of what the absolute idea is—or as Hegel also says—to an understanding of god.[148] It might thus be said that Hegel's *Logic* is a discovery of god's attributes.

The following may suffice to summarize the main points; they have been emphasized before, but they deserve restatement.

According to the absolute idea, subjectivity and objectivity—what is 'in itself' and 'for itself', and the theoretical and practical idea—are identical. To the empirical, limited, and finite consciousness, objectivity, the objective world, is viewed as something, as an "other," that is different from and independent of consciousness. To the universal, absolute mind, there is absolute identity between consciousness and its object. It is now understood that the view that the concepts of subject and object are distinct and mutually independent is erroneous: They are identical in the sense that both concepts are grasped or comprehended by, and are expressions of, identical categories. To put this differently: There is identity between

---

148. "Accordingly, logic is to be understood as the system of pure reason, as the realm of pure thought. This realm is truth as it is without veil and in its own absolute nature. It can therefore be said that this content is the exposition of god as he is in his eternal essence before the creation of nature and a finite mind" (*SL* 50).

thought and being. The subject has itself as an object, and, consequently, the object is the subject. The absolute idea has absolute freedom, simply because nothing outside it exists, and, therefore, nothing outside it or different from it can determine or influence it. (The concept of 'outside' has no meaning in connection with the absolute idea.)

The absolute idea incorporates the practical idea into the theoretical idea. Connected with the practical idea is the will. The will is defined in terms of its exercise as will, that is, as directed toward the attainment of an end. If there is no unattained end, there is no will.[149] Nevertheless, Hegel claims, the absolute idea unifies the practical and the theoretical idea. Hegel solves this problem (if he does solve it!) by saying that precisely by being united with cognition the will is now directed, not toward a not yet attained goal (because in the absolute idea nothing non-attained exists), but toward the cognition of what would have been a goal if it had not already been as it ought or should be.[150]

However, Hegel sometimes speaks about the absolute idea as if it were a being—a being who lives, thinks, and decides; this seems to imply a conscious being.[151] Being and thinking are identical; consequently, the absolute idea must have thought as an attribute; because thinking requires an object, that is, that which the thinking is about, the object for the absolute

---

149. "Therefore the will itself also requires that its purpose shall not be realized" (*Enz.* §234 Addition).

150. "The reconciliation consists in the will's returning—in its result—to the presupposition of cognition; hence the reconciliation consists in the unity of the theoretical and practical idea. The will knows the purpose as what is its own, and intelligence interprets the world as the concept in its actuality" (*Enz.* §234 Addition). It is difficult not to see this argument as, at best, unconvincing. It seems to imply that, so far as the absolute idea is concerned, the concept of the will is simply negated. Which, of course, it should be because the absolute idea cannot be regarded as having consciousness (and therefore a will), and because, furthermore, a will that is logically cut off from willing something cannot be called a will. But Hegel, so it seems, wants to preserve the concept of the will, and in so doing he changes it from being a will to being a cognitive concept.

151. One such statement is the following: "The absolute idea alone is being, imperishable life, self-knowing truth, and is all truth" (*SL* 824). And in §244 of the *Encyclopaedia*, he writes: "The absolute freedom of the idea, however, is that it does not merely pass over into life, nor that it lets life shine within itself as finite cognition, but that, in the absolute truth of itself, it resolves to release out of itself into freedom the moment of its particularity or of the initial determining and otherness, [i.e.], the immediate idea as its reflection, or itself as nature."

idea must be itself. In the universal consciousness, the subject has itself as object. Nevertheless, the absolute idea, the universal consciousness, must not be conceived as a consciousness over and above the innumerable empirical and finite consciousnesses. Only empirical and finite consciousness exists; no other form of consciousness can exist.

As just quoted (see note 148), Hegel asserts that his *Science of Logic* is to be understood as the system of pure reason—as the realm of pure thought. The content of this realm, Hegel further claims, is an exposition of god as he is in his eternal essence before the creation of nature and finite minds. In other words, god is conceived as a logical system. And a logical system cannot meaningfully be conscious. Furthermore, to say that god *creates* nature and finite minds must be taken to mean that the logical system constitutes the condition for the structure of nature and of any finite mind. Such a claim accords with the ontological nature of the categories—that is, the categories are categories not only for the subject but also for the object. Note that this is a condition of Hegel's basic thesis: that the truth should be conceived and expressed not only as substance, but also as subject. This is decisively different from the Kantian view, according to which the categories constitute the conditions for the thing in itself to be an object of experience—a view that precludes the thing in itself from ever being an object of experience.[152]

Thus Hegel's *Logic* is not only an investigation of pure reason, but it is also an investigation of the categories that determine the structure of whatever is (i.e., of being). Hegel's *Logic* is consequently also an ontology or, if one prefers, a metaphysical system.

Hegel, however, complains that metaphysical thinking is denigrated. He issues this warning: "Philosophy and ordinary common sense thus cooperating to bring about the downfall of metaphysics, thus was seen the strange spectacle of a cultured nation without metaphysics—like a temple richly ornamented in other aspects but without a holy of holies" (*SL* 25).

The problem, however, is not simply one of having a metaphysical system—it is part of human reason to have more or less cogent metaphysical views; those who reject the possibilities of a metaphysical system often do so on premises which themselves are rooted in metaphysical views. What is of greatest importance is whether the metaphysical view one

---

152. This is Hegel's conception of Kant's theory—a view he shares with many others. Nevertheless, such a view is neither the only nor necessarily the true interpretation of Kant' teachings; cf. my *Kant's Theory of Knowledge* (*op. cit.*), or my *History of Philosophy* (*op. cit.*).

accepts is based on sound arguments. That is, the arguments on which the system is based must be logically coherent, valid, and therefore not only acceptable but also unavoidable. Whether Hegel's metaphysical view is acceptable or perhaps even unavoidable depends on the arguments he brings forward. This is for the reader to decide. For my part I can say only that I have done my best to make it possible for the reader to pass judgment.

Summary

This final summary is not meant as a short-cut to the preceding pages, in case one has not yet read them, but to aid in forming an overview of the pages the patient reader has studied.

First, what does it mean to say that Hegel's *Logic* is about being? Obviously, the concept of being is not only the most fundamental ontological concept; it is the very concept expressing what we mean by the concept of ontology itself. A glance at the history of philosophy suffices to gain insight into the philosophical problems in ontology. From Heraclitus to Parmenides via Aristotle and Plato up to the time of Hegel, human thought has struggled with conflicting views of the nature of being.

Hegel's contribution to ontology is, among other things, the way he dealt with ontological problems. Instead of saying, as it often is said, that he deduces the concepts (the categories) that are necessary for understanding the concept of being, it is more correct to say that Hegel attempts by philosophical analysis to find the rules of deep grammar governing ontological thinking and, therefore, ontological language. This way of articulating Hegel's contribution emphasizes the therapeutic element that is basic to his *Logic*.

Hegel's first rule of deep grammar concerns the concept of negation; this concept in turn is connected with the concept of identity. Hegel distinguishes formal or empty identity—an identity he calls nonsense. To say that "a planet is a planet" is, as Wittgenstein says, to let language idle. Valid identity, on the other hand, is concrete identity, the identity about which it is correct to say that a thing is—its identity conditions are determined by—what it is not. To say that a thing is red is to say that it is neither yellow, green, blue, nor any other color. It is thus identical with the negation of all the colors that it does not have. To say that a person is courageous is to say that she or he is not a coward. And to say that a person is intelligent, is to say that she or he is what she or he is not. She or he is neither stupid, feeble minded, nor retarded.

The rule of negation avoids conceptual conflicts involving bad infinity, namely that infinity which moves from 'something' to 'something else' to 'some third thing' and so on to infinity. When something is identical with what it is not (that is, when the identity conditions of one thing are determined by those for something else), then the conceptual movement is from 'something' to the negation of this 'something', which is precisely identical with itself. Whereas bad infinity is the straight line continued into infinity (which is logically tied to the finite), true infinity is a circle expressing self-relation.

The rule of negation therefore implies the rule of deep grammar Hegel calls being-for-self. By this rule, one likewise avoids the problems (or rather the pseudo-problems) connected with bad infinity. The being-for-self rule leads to the rule of reciprocity, the application of which leads to, among other things, the identity between substance and accidents, between force and expressions, between inner and outer, and between cause and effect. Without the rule of reciprocity, the relation of cause and effect leads to bad infinity; according to the rule of reciprocity, they are identical: The effect is identical with the negation of the cause (the cause is identical with that which it is not). One cannot distinguish between cause and effect; they, so to speak, fuse together (cf. Crawford Elder's remark, quoted in note 100); at the moment of fusing, neither of the two concepts can be given any meaning.

The rule of reciprocity entails that everything is related to everything else. Or, rather, to understand something is to understand it as part of a whole, as an element in a system. The rule of reciprocity (which derives from being-for-self, which in turn presupposes negation, or that everything *is* determined by what it is not) entails, as we have seen, that the two elements of cognition (substance and accident, force and expression, cause and effect, outer and inner, etc.) logically fuse together and become conceptually indistinguishable. They are not distinct, individual empirical data. There is no empirical datum one can call, for instance, 'the' cause or 'the' force and its expressions, etc. Instead, one deals in concepts. Hence we are no longer confronted by, for example, Hume's problem. There are not, as Hume maintains, two events: a cause and an effect. It is therefore a pseudo-problem if one attempts in experience to find a connection between them.

That does not mean, however, that it has been an error to use concepts, such as the concept of causation. There evidently have been errors in conceiving the relation between cause and effect, such as Hume's. What this does mean is that the concepts of cause and effect, purified by means of the rule of deep grammar, are sublated in the concept.

I shall not recapitulate here Hegel's route from the concept to the absolute idea—a route outlined above—but shall only say this: As noted already in the "Preface" to the *Phenomenology,* Hegel held that everything depends on showing that truth can be expressed both as substance (that is, object) and as subject. In the absolute idea, all the concepts of logic (the rules of deep grammar), purified by philosophical analysis, are sublated. The absolute idea is the unity of subject and object, of the finite and the truly infinite. To the extent that thinking pertains to the absolute idea, the object of thinking is—as Aristotle held—its own thinking. In order to avoid an infinite regress, one may interpret both Aristotle's and Hegel's statements about the thinking of the unmoved mover or the absolute idea (respectively), such that this thinking, which is one's own thinking, is a consciousness of thinking. To say that one is conscious of thinking is plainly not unproblematic (cf. Gilbert Ryle's *The Concept of Mind,* for instance). All the same, I make this statement here because of its current salience: In his recent book *The Shadow of the Mind,* professor of mathematics at Oxford University Roger Penrose thinks he can prove that an artificial intelligence, however well-construed, never will attain that which characterizes human intelligence (namely awareness of thinking).

As I mentioned in the Foreword, the history of philosophy—even a history of philosophy that omits all the philosophers who are not regarded as having contributed to the progress of philosophy—cannot be represented in a straight line. Without undue repetition, let me stress the following: One cannot draw a straight line, for instance, from Hume to Kant or from Kant to Hegel. Hegel has shown that cause and effect are not two distinct events, but are instead fused events. This fusion, furthermore, cannot even be characterized as an event in time. About a billiard ball which has been hit we can say at a given time "Now it rolls," but that statement by necessity implies the statement "It has started rolling."

A crucial difference between Kant and Hegel is that, whereas Kant's categories presuppose transcendental apperception and therefore imply "the thing in itself," Hegel's unqualified beginning is the fundamental concept of ontology, the concept of being. Logic is therefore a conceptual determination of this concept. There is thus no logical place for any in principle unknowable thing in itself.

Hegel clearly is subject to criticism. But one thing is certain: Hegel cannot be disregarded.

Bibliography

Hegel's work is the subject of a great number of studies, most of which, however, deal with parts of Hegel's philosophy other than his logic. The following list is limited to works I have found useful in general and works I have found useful in writing the present book.

Brøchner, Hans, *Philosophiens Historie* I–II, København: Gyldendalske Boghandel, 1873–74.

Clark, Malcolm, *Logic and System*, The Hague: Nijhoff, 1971.

Copleston, Frederick, *History of Philosophy*, vol. VII, Garden City: Image Books, 1963.

Elder, Crawford, *Appropriating Hegel*, Aberdeen: Aberdeen University Press, 1980.

Fischer, Kuno, *Hegels Leben, Werke und Lehre*, Erster Teil, Heidelberg: Carl Winters Universitätsbuchhandlung, 1911.

Gadamer, Hans-Georg, *Hegel's Dialectic: Five Hermeneutic Studies*, New Haven: Yale University Press, 1976.

Harris, Errol E., *An Interpretation of The Logic of Hegel*, Lanham: University Press of America, 1983.

————, *Formal, Transcendental and Dialectical Thinking: Logic and Reality*, Albany: SUNY Press, 1987.

Johnson, Paul Owen, *The Critique of Thought: A Re-examination of Hegel's Science of Logic*, Brookfield, VT: Gower Publishing Company, 1988.

Hyppolite, Jean, *Studies on Marx and Hegel*, New York: Basic Books, 1969.

Kaufmann, Walter, *Hegel, Reinterpretation, Texts, and Commentary*, New York: Doubleday, 1965.

Lakebrink, Bernhard, *Kommentar zu Hegels Logik in seiner Enzyklopädie von 1830*, I–II, Freiburg & München: Alber, 1979, 1985.

McTaggart, J.E.M., *A Commentary on Hegel's Logic*, Cambridge: Cambridge University Press, 1910.

Mure, G.R.G., *A Study of Hegel's Logic*, London: Oxford University Press, 1967.

Pippin, Robert B., *Hegel's Idealism*, Cambridge: Cambridge University Press, 1989.

Stace, W.T., *The Philosophy of Hegel*, London: Macmillan, 1923.

Taylor, Charles, *Hegel*, Cambridge: Cambridge University Press, 1975.